Release Me:

My Life, My Words

Release Me:

My Life, My Words

Olivia Longott

www.urbanbooks.net

Urban Books, LLC
97 N18th Street
Wyandanch, NY 11798

Release Me: My Life, My Words Copyright © 2014
Olivia Longott

ISBN 13: 978-1-60162-416-1
ISBN 10: 1-60162-416-6

First Trade Paperback Printing July 2014
Printed in the United States of America

10 9 8 7 6 5 4 3 2 1

All pictures were provided by the Author.

Photographs taken by LeMar L. Joichin III
www.LeMarJphoto.com

Distributed by Kensington Publishing Corp.
Submit Wholesale Orders to:
Kensington Publishing Corp.
C/O Penguin Group (USA) Inc.
Attention: Order Processing
405 Murray Hill Parkway
East Rutherford, NJ 07073-2316
Phone: 1-800-526-0275
Fax: 1-800-227-9604

Release Me:

My Life, My Words

by

Olivia Longott

"The First Lady of G-Unit"
−50 Cent

Dedication

My biggest inspiration is my grandmother, Celeste Blake. I have watched you raise four beautiful daughters and one son, who then turned around and raised amazing children of their own. You have always been a woman of faith, strength, and courage. Whether you know it or not, I aspire to be you. We celebrated your 90th birthday in our country, Jamaica, and in your home on September 23, 2013. Grandpa is smiling down on all of us with a glass of cognac in his hand. Family will always be a top priority to me.

I dedicate this book to every person in my family who never gave up and pushed themselves to accomplish their dreams, and to those still striving. My mom started out as a school teacher in Jamaica and my father drove big rig trailers in Jamaica. They came to the U.S. very young and made great career paths for themselves. I have seen them both work long hours to provide for our family. All of my attributes I obtained from them both. I would not be the strong, faithful, intelligent, God fearing, beautiful woman I am today without them. More than thirty-two years of marriage and the best example of a loving home I could have ever asked for. To family!

Acknowledgments

I can do all things through Christ who strengthens me. —Philippians 4:13

I want to thank Carl Weber for giving me the opportunity to broaden my horizons. I have been putting my book together for the past two years. To see everything coming together before my eyes is absolutely wonderful. I am thankful for the opportunity to tell my story through my own words and eyes.

I am a very private person, but doing this book has given me the courage to open up more. Everyone has a story to tell. I only hope to captivate you, the reader, with my words so that you understand "Olivia" in your own way.

I would also like to thank Tony Gakins Jr. for pushing me to tell my story. I was only interested in writing children's books, but you convinced me that I had much more to share. Your belief in my talents is what started this book-writing journey, and I thank you for that.

"Down But Not Out"

In life we all have choices;
It's not an easy path.
I wish that we could snap our fingers and have inside
our hearts
what lingers,
Longing for that one great dream,
The one you've dreamt a million times
That in reality it seems
You're not quite at the finish line.
You do your best
But always feel that someone's always better.
It's not that they're ahead of you;
You've just got some more work to do.
See, God has placed you on this earth
For purpose and with reason.
Not that you won't get your shine;
It's not your time or season.
I know you've heard He gives it to you only when you're
ready,
So practice hard at what you do,
Stay strong and be steady.
I know at times you feel so down,
Like nothing is going to work,

But if you just believe in you
And all the magnificent things you can do,
I promise you will show yourself

"Down But Not Out"

That you are so much better;
Better than you thought you were,
Better now than ever.
So don't feel bad you're not there yet;
Your time's around the corner.
You may be down, but you're not out;
You're a fighter, that, I have no doubt.
So stand your ground, your head held high,
With confidence look to the sky.

-Olivia T. Longott

02/18/2020

Item(s) Checked Out

TITLE   Release me : my life,
BARCODE   33029070901426
DUE DATE   **03-10-20**

TITLE   The cartel 3 : the last
BARCODE   33029105317341
DUE DATE   **03-10-20**

Total Items This Session: 2

Terminal #   18

Prologue

I was molested when I was five years old, and my daddy abandoned me when I was seven. My mother was addicted to crack cocaine by the time I was ten, so my grandma had to raise me. I ended up with a baby by the time I was fifteen, had two abortions by the time I was eighteen, and stayed with my abusive boyfriend until he ended up getting sentenced to life on a murder charge. After that, the strip club became my home. My baby and I had to eat, didn't we?

I know that is the kind of life that makes people's eyes pop, that intrigues them and makes them want to delve deeper into someone's world in order to find out every raw, grimy, and painful detail of the person's past. Unfortunately that is someone's story, but it's not mine.

My prayer is for once in my lifetime somebody wants to know the details of the happily-ever-after story. That someone will say to their misery, "No, you can't have company tonight." That for once people will open up their minds to just plain old *happy* and know that it does exist . . . without pain being its predecessor. Yes, I've endured pain, failures, and losses, but the good definitely outweighs the bad.

What I've learned through all that I've endured is that everything doesn't have to be all bad in order to eventually get to the good. It's a fifty-fifty thing. Stuff can either start off bad and then get good, or start off good and then go bad. But I have to admit that there is always that infamous threat of from-bad-to-worse hanging in limbo, and I wouldn't be telling the truth if I said I haven't experienced a few of those instances in my life.

I try to always focus on the good, though. I guess it's safe to say that I'm a glass-half-full kind of girl, but then there are always those thirsty people in life who come around just to suck up every drop out of the glass anyway. Still, I choose to focus on the positive and believe that no matter how anything starts off or ends, like a Tootsie Roll Pop, there is something good in the middle of it all. The test is seeing if you can survive long enough to get to the good stuff. The struggle shouldn't make us bitter, but make us better.

You know, I often hear church folk say, "Well, you know that if it doesn't come with a struggle, then it ain't of God." I refuse to believe the God I serve and everything about Him has hurt, pain, and struggle attached. I've seen things fall into place when done right. Heck, I've seen things fall into place when done wrong. Whether I'm doing it right or wrong, I guess that's still to be determined.

Some things have come easy in my life. Some things came with obstacles and detours, while some have yet to come at all. While others choose to Facebook their problems, I choose to face mine. And, yes, I do have problems. Whether they are deemed big or small, shallow or deep, I don't care. I'm not here to compare my wounds to anybody else's. I'm not here to see whose journey was the longest, roughest, and hardest. I'm just here to finish the damn journey. So, in the words of Jerry McGuire, "Who's coming with me?"

Chapter 1

Taking care of people has always made me happy. It's like it soothed my soul. If everybody else around me is feeling and doing good, then so am I. There is something about putting a smile on someone's face with the simplest gesture that makes my day. On the low, I am a bit emotional, but you wouldn't know that unless you were in my inner circle. I can recall when I was around five years old, wanting to always help my mother in any way possible just to make her happy. She worked for a real estate company in Long Island, New York, and to me it felt like she was there all day. I would miss her so much all day that I couldn't wait for her to come waltzing through that door.

My older brother, Christopher, would be upstairs somewhere playing music and watching karate movies, while I was anxiously waiting to hear the sound of her car pull up in the driveway. I'd already rehearsed in my head a thousand times all I was going to tell her about my day. The majority of the time my dad got in at later hours because he was a manager at JFK Airport, so it would just be me waiting there at the door to try my best to wipe away that tired, drained look on my mother's face or give her more joy, depending on what kind of day she'd had.

"Hi, Mommy." I'd wrap my arms around her waist, squeezing my eyes closed just as tightly as I was squeezing her. She could barely even make it in the door.

"Hey, my Livy," she would reply, the exhaustion in her tone not undetected by even a five-year-old.

"Can I get you anything, Mommy?"

"No, my baby. I'm good." She sighed and then made her way over to the couch, dropping her purse and keys on the coffee table.

"How 'bout a pillow to put your feet on top of?" I eagerly suggested, grabbing one of the throw pillows from the couch. Trying to fluff up the pillow, I said, "I saw this daddy on a television show I was watching do it for the mommy. It made her smile."

I sat there impatiently waiting for her to give me an order, any order, that my accomplishing would please her. Then it happened. A smile crept across her face as she rubbed my cheek with the back of her hand.

"Yes, dear, you know I love when you do that, but I'm going to make us both some tea first." She knew I loved hot tea, but of course I was too young to make it by myself. I always felt like such a grown-up sitting there sipping tea with my mom like I had me some business.

"Can I help you make the tea, Mommy? Please."

"Sure, Livy." Just as tired as all get out, she slowly lifted herself from the couch.

I tossed that pillow right back on the couch, and with a matching smile now on my face, I took my mother by the hand and led her downstairs into the kitchen.

We lived in a two-family home that had three levels. The kitchen was in the basement, along with the dining room. I released her hand to do my famous slide across the kitchen floor. I always loved sliding across the tiles in my socks. The tiles were beige to offset the matte white cabinets. Most of the décor in our home was lighter colors. That always made our home feel so open and bright.

Once my mother assisted me in getting the tea prepared, I made her sit at the kitchen table, and as if I were the adult, I tried to tend to her by putting sugar in her cup. "One lump or two?" I would mimic everything I heard on

TV—and I would try to say it with a British accent. Don't ask me why; I was just different.

My mother would sit there watching me. I would just be talking my head off like she was one of my classmates who understood the language of a kindergartner.

While she sipped the tea, I would sometimes read a book to her. Other times, I would make up these grand stories off the top of my head to tell her.

When I was actually reading to her from one of my favorite books, I can remember glancing up in between pauses to stare at her. My mother always looked so pretty. I admired her grace and beauty. She wore the prettiest long, silk skirts and tops, and she always had a belt around her small waist. No one could tell my mother she wasn't styling. Oh, and when her hair was flipped like Farrah Fawcett, that was a whole other story. I paid attention to every detail.

I know that's where I get my love of hairstyles from. Whenever I'm sitting in the mirror doing my hair, it's almost as if I'm looking at my mother in the mirror. I looked just like my mom when she was my age. That's why when I see myself, I can't help but see her.

Although I had lots of friends, I enjoyed spending time with my mother the most. She and I used to go for walks. To this day I can still hear her singing, "Skip to my Lou, My Darling," as I pranced down the block in my little pink jelly shoes.

"Freeze!" she would yell out.

That's when I would stop and pose. I held that pose so hard, with my hands on my hips and a Zoolander facial expression. Oh my gosh, she loved that. She would just clap and smile up to the heavens. Not me. I'd be concentrating hard, with a fierce look on my face, while striking a pose like I was in a Madonna video or something.

I loved to dress up, and once I got older, I always switched my style up. I remember these one pair of shorts distinctively. I think I wore those little blue short shorts with white trim on the bottom to the park every week. My hair was braided back all fly, and I wore a blue T-shirt to match and of course some jellies. I was the jelly shoes princess. Back in the 1980s those were what was up, and nobody could tell me that I wasn't the freshest kid on the playground.

We would pull up on our bikes at the park. It was like six of us: my brother and his friend, two girls from my neighborhood, and me and my bestie. I liked wearing my hair braided all back in eight cornrows, looking like Queen Latifah in the movie *Set It Off*. Even rolling on my bike, while everyone else had on their kicks, I still had on those damn pink jellies. I just had to be different, even then.

There were days where I felt like being extra fancy, so my mom would put me in knee-length dresses and would have my hair in a high ponytail to the side with a bow in it. Match that with my white lace ruffled socks and shiny black shoes, and *ooh wee!* I was sharp enough to cut the sidewalk!

When I look back at our family photos, my mom had me in an awful lot of dresses. I feel like every dress was white or had white in it and had some type of lace frills on it. She always had me looking right, I must admit. In almost every picture I was doing this one pose that my mom still does to this day. Everyone in my family knows there is only one way my mother takes a picture. I would have one hand on my hip and the other straight down to my side, with my foot pointing out. Y'all know that pose. It's that "Ta-dah! Look at me!" pose. I was so girlie. So how ironic is it that I turned out to be a tomboy?

I used to always chill with my crew on Springfield Boulevard. I hung with these guys that called themselves "Crum Corp." Don't even ask me what the hell that meant. I didn't choose the name. Anyway, we used to kick it in front of my boy Bubba Smith's house, or over at my favorite crazy guy Tank's house.

Bubba was the rapper of the crew, and so was my best friend Bingo. Bingo is still my boy to this day. Man, he used to get me in so much trouble; I can't even believe I still mess with that fool. Bingo and I hung around each other so much that people used to think we were brother and sister. If someone was looking for either of us, they knew where to find us: his house or my house. I don't know how we didn't drive Bingo's parents and grandparents crazy. I would sometimes be over his house at the crack of dawn. Bingo always got up early, which meant he called me to come over early to write and record or to cause trouble.

It was cool for us to hang out at each other's houses until late at night or until the wee hours in the morning, but if it got too late, our parents were there to remind us. All we'd be doing was rapping and singing and cooking—which reminds me of his grandma's slammin' turkey burgers. She loved making us those darn burgers, and we'd be sitting at the kitchen table ready to devour them. Bingo had built a home studio in the basement. We had sheets on the walls to try to stop sound from coming in. The mic was cheap, but hey, it could record. Bingo also had an MPC machine to make beats. We were always serious about our craft, even way back then.

I don't remember any of the guys having steady girl-friends, so I didn't have to deal with catty girls being mad that their boyfriends were always around me. Besides, everyone knew we were all just friends. We were like the Junior Mafia of Queens. I loved those guys. They would refer to me as "Queen" all the time. They always had my back.

I can't forget my boy Bundy. We used to chill at his spot on occasion as well. Bundy and I went to high school together, and he was part of the crew too. Bundy actually became my hype man on stage when I really got into the music and started having bigger shows. Bundy would be on stage dancing and back-flipping. When I tell y'all he used to be turnt-up on them stages . . . *Man!* Not only was this the crew I got into trouble with, but they also taught me how to shoot my first gun. More trouble!

One day we were all at Bubba's crib just talking about school, parties and whatnot. Sometimes we would rap in a cypher (I was nice as hell) and occasionally sip some Patrón. Now that I think back, I suppose Patrón has always been my drink of choice, not that I had any business sipping anything besides iced tea back then. I was around sixteen or seventeen at the time.

"Yo, wassup? Anybody down for target practice?" Bubba asked as he came downstairs, where we were all hanging out, with his chest all puffed up, ready for a little show and tell.

"Man, what the hell are you talking about now?" Tank said while sipping on some Hennessy, his drink of choice. Tank was the oldest of the crew; two years older than the rest of us.

Tank was the one who got us liquor. Don't ask me how, but when he was around, a bottle of Hennessy would always magically appear. Tank was also the one who loved to start trouble. His nickname was Tank for a reason: he was built like one and dared anyone to step to him. He was so amusing to watch. He was one of those guys who talked all the crap in the world but could back up every word. Yeah, that was Tank.

"I got a little ounish you guys might want to check out," Bubba said.

We called everything and everyone an "ounish." It was our own made-up word. We'd be like, "Wassup, Oun Oun," or "I got the ounish wit' me." You know; our own language.

"Yo, this guy is crazy." I laughed. "He always got some new stuff he wanna show us." I looked to Bubba. "Yeah, we wanna see, Bub."

Bubba turned and pulled from behind him a Mack 10.

"Holy crap! This guy wasn't joking," Tank said as he spit out his sip of Hennessy in shock. "Man, put that cannon away."

"No, let me see, man," I asked curiously.

"You sure you can handle this much steel?" Bubba said, raising his eyebrows. He used to do that thing with his eyebrow long before The Rock made the facial expression famous.

"Boy, if you don't give me that damn gun . . ." I said.

"All right, all right." Bubba handed me the gun.

I held it up in a shooting position, like I was Angelina Jolie in that movie *Mr. & Mrs. Smith*. I wasn't a stranger to or afraid of guns. My father had a gun, but he never let me see or handle it. It was locked away in his closet, so I was way too excited to get my paws on this one. "Where the hell did you get this from? Better question: where can we go to try it out?" I said, intrigued by the deadly weapon. I was always too dayum hype to get into some trouble.

"What? Liv wanna pop off the steel too?" Bubba joked as I sucked my teeth. "All right, I'm done messing with you. No problem."

"You gon' let her play wit' it for real?" Tank asked Bubba with his eyebrows now raised.

"Liv? Hell yeah. She one of the boys." Bubba shrugged.

"All right then," Tank said, shaking his head. "But hold up."

Tank headed up the steps and called for Bingo to come with him. Within seconds they had both disappeared up the steps. When they returned, I think they had collected every phone book Bubba had in the house.

"Help us set these up, y'all," Tank ordered.

Bubba, Bingo, Tank, and I set up the phone books, one on top of the other, for our bootleg target practice. What made this even worse was that we were shooting right next to the boiler, so if we had missed the books and hit the boiler, I would not be writing this book right now. Thank God Bubba's mom wasn't home from work yet. Then again, maybe she could have stopped our dumb asses from what we were about to try.

"Let me go first." I held onto that gun like I knew what the hell I was doing. I closed my left eye tightly while squinting my right eye, trying to focus so that I could get a good aim; then I squeezed the trigger. The force of the gun shifted my body back a bit, but once the bullet was released, I was still standing. Come to think of it, no matter what them fools got me caught up in, I was always still standing. And when I say I was always caught up in something with the crew, that's exactly what I mean.

Them dudes always had me up to no good. There was this one time when it was just me and Bingo and his boy Devi. Bingo and I left Devi upstairs while we went to make sandwiches downstairs. Bingo must have left his gun out in plain sight, because needless to say, we heard the gun go off. Bingo and I immediately went into our crazy, silly panic mode.

"Holy shit! Was that what I think it was, Batman?" Bingo said, nervous as hell, looking at me.

"Why, yes. Yes it was, Robin!" I responded. We dropped the plates on the table and flew up the stairs. Bingo and I joked all the time; we couldn't help it. We pulled lines from different movies and used it in our everyday conversations.

Although we heard the gun go off, we didn't hear Devi screaming, so we pretty much knew he hadn't foolishly shot himself. The question was what or where did he shoot at? God forbid he aimed at a window and an innocent bystander was walking by. High dudes and guns definitely don't mix.

"What the hell happened? We heard the gun go off," I said to Devi, all out of breath.

Devi was just sitting there staring up at the ceiling with this dumb smile on his face. Devi always, I mean always, had a smile on his face. It didn't matter what time of day it was or what was going on around him; that boy kept a smile on his face. I'm sure it was partly because he always smoked weed, but hey, at least he always smiled. We didn't know if he was in shock or what.

Next thing I knew, Bingo went over to Devi and started patting him down. "You all right, man? You hit?"

Devi started shoving Bingo's hands off of him. When I say these two Negroes looked like they were having a fly-swatting contest, I am not exaggerating.

"Man, get off of me. I'm good," Devi tried to tell Bingo to no avail.

By this time, I was cracking up looking at Ren and Stimpy. Even Devi busted out laughing. All the while Bingo was as serious as a heart attack, still patting down his boy to see if he came across blood or anything.

"Man, the bullet ain't in me. It's up there." Devi pointed up to the ceiling where he had been staring, while at the same time managing to slap Bingo's hands away. Those two were classic.

We were all looking up at the ceiling where the bullet sat lodged in the drywall.

"See, I'm cool, man," Devi assured Bingo, still laughing.

Now Bingo's concern turned to anger. "How the hell you gon' shoot a gun off in the crib and not warn anybody? What if Liv and me were walking up the stairs and ya aim was off?" He stopped to take a breather and calm down. "You know what? It's my fault, 'cause I shouldn't have left the gun out for you to see anyway," Bingo said. "I know your ass likes guns. I should have known better with your happy high ass," he continued.

"Shit, I didn't know the safety was off. I was just messing around. When I pulled the trigger I didn't expect a bullet to go flying."

Bingo shook his head and snatched the gun from him, putting the safety back on.

"Damn, man, my bad," Devi said. "I would have never shot it had I known it—"

"Wasn't on safety. We know, we know," I said, finishing Devi's sentence for him.

"No," he said, "if I had known I was going to get felt up by your boy."

Devi and I laughed our butts off. Even Bingo had to laugh at that one. Man, I wish camera phones and YouTube were in then. That scene would have gone viral.

"Oh my God, we can't leave you alone for a second." I shook my head

"Man, you could have killed yourself . . . or shot your eye out, kid," Bingo added.

Man, we all held our stomachs laughing so hard after Bingo's line from that movie, *A Christmas Story*.

I loved hanging with those fools, though. Never a dull moment. Even when I was younger I had more fun with boys. The majority of my cousins were boys, and they were always at the house romping around. Rory and Kurt are my mom's closest sister's kids. They lived at the opposite end of the block from us. You can best believe that play dates were daily; from video games to playing with Mask and GI Joe to riding our bikes. Uncle Courtney, who is my mom's sister's husband, used to make Rory and me peanut butter and jelly sandwiches with melted cheese on the inside. I know it sounds weird, but don't knock it until you try it. I don't know who came up with that combination, but trust me, it tastes outstanding.

Even though I would wild out with the fellas, that didn't keep me from playing with my little girl friends. While most of them wanted to play with toys or jump Double Dutch, I'd be the one always wanting to sing to the toys or to my friends. I definitely joined in to play Double Dutch, but I still made a song out of it somehow. As a very young child, I was fearless when it came to the spotlight being on me. I would always look for ways to entertain people, and if no one was around, I'd just entertain myself. I had this one Barbie I know I drove my mom crazy with. It was a Rock and Roll Barbie, and I would sing into the hairbrush that came along as one of Barbie's accessories.

"Born with the mic in my hand, singing everything that I can, born with the mic in my hand," I would belt out. That probably was one of my first "ah-ha" moments when I thought, *Hey, I'm good at this.* I had to be eight years old then.

The older I got, though, the more I became plagued with this whole shyness thing.

My mom always sang around the house or in the church choir, so at times when I wasn't being my shy self, I would join her. I know people hear stories about how entertainers are so shy until they hit the stage and it's time to sing. Well, with me, even when I hit the stage and opened my mouth, I was still shy as all get out. I would even make people turn their backs to me when I sang.

I was indeed comfortable with singing and was more than in my element when doing so. The difference for me, though, was that singing was just so personal to me. It was a vocal diary of some sort. It was like it was a gift from God; my own personal little island in this big ol' crazy world. So I'd close my eyes, open my mouth, and it would be just me and my voice that lived there on the island; no one else. As long as there was no one else, there were no worries and fears.

It wasn't until I started singing in the church choir myself that I broke out of my shyness a little bit. People's reaction to the big voice coming out of such a small body was my wake-up call that I couldn't hold my talent captive on the island. My speaking voice was so raspy that people were shocked my singing voice had such a beautiful tone to it. But God forbid if the choir director asked me to do a solo. I would be a nervous wreck!

I would practice with a few girls from my church every Wednesday and Friday. Siobhonne, Shaniqua, Tyesha, and I were in the same age group and a part of the youth choir. Alexis and her sister Porsha were older than us, but they treated me like their little sister. They took me under their wings and tried to break me out of my shyness. That would help me out a bit because we sang as a group, so I never really had to endure the spotlight just being on me.

Anything that singled me out was hard on my nerves. I was such a perfectionist and would sing things over and over until I felt I got it right. I would always try to get my vocals to blend and fit in with the other girls. Siobhonne and I would sing on our front porches every day when we got in from school. She lived next door to me. If we saw someone coming down the block, instead of trying to show off and put on a show, we sang quieter until they passed by us—which made no sense, because we were so loud. I know they heard us all the way down the block. We were a piece of work!

Our best moments were down in Siobhonne's aunt's basement, where we played records by our favorite artists or groups: SWV, Escape, En Vogue, Mary J. Blige, and more. We would sing our faces off as if no one could hear us. We sounded great, but still my voice just never seemed to blend in. That's when I realized that maybe, just maybe, I wasn't born to fit in, but born to stand out.

For the rest of my teen years, the whole blending in and standing out issue bothered me just that much more. I was so self-conscious, always aware of how I sounded or looked.

I remember my music director at Bayside High School asking me to sing the lead in one of our performances. Because I was so shy and worried I'd mess up, I turned it down. The girl who ended up doing the lead did a great job. The crowd went crazy, and it led to some other things for her. I was so mad at myself for not just trying. I could have done it. I had sung the song a million times at home and in the car, but my nerves and fear of messing up always got the best of me.

I remember crying myself to sleep the night of the concert and praying to God, "Please, God, give me strength so that fear never gets in my way again of getting something that I want—something that belongs to me."

I closed my eyes and could only hope that God had heard my prayer . . . and would answer it. The last thing I wanted or needed was to get in my own way.

Chapter 2

When I say being shy was like a phobia, I'm not exaggerating. I just wish I'd had my mother to help encourage and talk me through it. With the way things were looking between my mother and me, you could file that under *N* for *not gonna happen*!

When I was younger my mother was like my best friend. It seemed like the older I got, the more distance there was between us. The days of her coming in from work and sitting down at the kitchen table talking with me over tea were scarce. As a matter of fact, once I was in my teens, I didn't have much conversation with my mom at all. By then I was more of a daddy's little girl.

I often wondered how my grandmother had raised my mom. Like, why was she so private about everything? And so conservative? Not that being conservative is a problem, but sometimes you have to let your hair down. You feel me? I just can't imagine my grandmother being so soft-spoken with raising her kids. My grandmother is a firecracker! To this day, at ninety years old, she is still talking crap and drinking her Guinness and Malta.

My mom is the total opposite. She doesn't like loud noise, arguing, or confrontation. She can't even take guns going off in movies. Do you know the amount of times she made my dad change the channel when we were watching a violent movie? Just peace and quiet, a cup of tea, and the Word Channel for her.

I love that my mom is such a peaceful spirit, but some-times you gotta speak up for yourself. I really needed her to be present when I was a teen. Those are the times when a girl needs to talk to her mother the most. I was anything but reserved. I was quiet at times, but definitely not reserved. Perhaps if I'd been less aggressive as a teen and learned how to tone it down, she might have felt like she could have a conversation with me. I just wish she would have been more understanding as to how different the times were for me growing up than when she and her siblings did.

When I was little, I talked to my mom all the time. I could ask her any and everything that came to my mind. One time, while we were in the family room, I asked my mom what happens to us when we die. I had to be like ten years old.

My mom was stumped, because every response she gave me I would in turn ask her, "Why?"

Those days of chit chatting with my mother became a distant memory. There was so much I wanted to share, tell, and ask my mother, but she never really opened up to me. I felt like I was on an island all right, but my mother was on a totally different one. Slowly but surely, the two islands drifted apart.

It affected me a lot. The majority of my friends' or boy-friends' mothers were so easy to talk to. I found myself wishing I could have conversations with my own mom like the ones I had with them. I never wanted another mom; I just wanted my own to be more open with me.

Whenever my mother felt a need to express herself, it was always through letters. My mother was raised very old fashioned by my Jamaican grandparents. West Indian parents have different ways of parenting that my mother just never seemed to break away from, I guess. Her other sisters were very open with their kids, though.

Out of five siblings, two of them were private, and my mom happened to be one of the private ones. I could never have an intimate conversation with my mom. Don't let a kissing scene or anything halfway sexual come on television when she was around either. That channel would get turned so quick. I think it was just to avoid me asking her questions and her having to answer them.

I don't even remember if she was the first person I told when I got my period. There were a lot of unspoken things between us. I honestly think the conversation of me starting my period with my mother consisted of, "Mom, can you buy me some pads?" I had to learn about sex and having a period from my brother's girlfriend, Libbe, who was four years older than me.

My mother and I never discussed my having a period, what to do and not do. We never had a discussion about the birds and the bees. It always felt awkward if I tried to initiate a conversation along those lines. I wouldn't even know what to say to my mom about my first sexual experience. How do you even start that conversation? "Hey, Mom, guess what I did today?" I can only imagine the look on her face if I'd said something like that to her. She probably would have doused me with holy water and oil, then started praying over me. That mother in the old *Carrie* movie wouldn't have had nothing over my moms! All I can say is thank the heavens for older cousins, best friends, and big sister figures like Alexis and Libbe, or I never would have known about a lot of things a growing teenage girl needs to know.

Even if my mom was proud of me, it was rare for her to say those words. I only knew she was proud of me after reading it in one of her letters. Sometimes I would be so grateful for those uplifting letters. They would be just what I needed at times. But then there were the not so encouraging letters—the hurtful ones. Let's just say that most of the time when those came, I wasn't always in a good mental place.

I recall coming in late from the studio with my first cousin, Paul, who always took me to and from the studio. I'd started going to the studio with my older brother, Christopher. I would join his rap sessions with his boys. He was older, and then there was the fact that he was a boy, so he was allowed to hang out at the studio much later than I was, so I couldn't ride with him all the time. But I managed to get in where I fit in. Having cousin Paulie there by my side pretty much made it easier.

"Thanks for giving me a ride, Paulie." My mom had given him the nickname "Paul Potato," but I wasn't calling him that. That nickname was so weak; she was on her own with that one. Paulie was all the nickname he was going to get from me. We stepped inside my house.

"You killed it in the studio tonight," Paul said.

"You think so?" I smiled.

"Stop being modest. You know you were on fire."

"Yeah, I was, wasn't I?" I agreed and then laughed.

"Well, I'm going to head on home."

"You want something to drink before you go?"

"Yeah, I am a little parched." He let out this fake cough with his crazy self.

"Don't you think I'm the one who should be parched after using my voice for hours?" I shook my head. "Come on, boy." I laughed as I led him into the kitchen. Upon turning on the light switch, my heart rate immediately picked up. Sitting smack dead in the middle of the kitchen table was a white sheet of paper nicely folded, with bold letters that simply read: Olivia.

In my head I was like, *Okay, Olivia, it can't be that bad.* I figured that maybe she was just telling me that she left dinner in the fridge for me or to make sure I turned out all the lights before I went upstairs to bed. Then my thoughts started to see the cup as half empty. Perhaps she was going to get on me about coming in so late. Whatever was written in the letter, I knew I wasn't going to read it in front of Paul.

"What's wrong?" Paul asked as he began frantically looking around. "Roaches don't come out when y'all turn the lights on, do they?"

Not even one of Paul's silly comments could thaw out my frozen state. I couldn't even give him a "You so crazy." I just shook my head.

"Then what do y'all have to drink?" Paul brushed by me and went to the refrigerator, scanned it, and then retrieved a can of soda. He cracked it open and took a huge sip. "That hit the spot. Thank you, Mommy," he said, using the same nickname my dad had for me. "Now let me hit the road."

"All right. Thanks again," I said to Paul, but still focused on the letter. "Be sure to lock that bottom lock."

Just as soon as Paul exited the kitchen, I darn near tripped over my feet in an attempt to get to the letter. I picked it up, unfolded it, and began to read.

I hope you are not out playing with boys late at night and just using that whole studio business as an excuse. I know there are boys there. I pray the enemy is not trying to use them as a distraction from what you are called to do. If you were doing it in the church, glorifying God with your voice, then there wouldn't even be this opportunity for the devil to use you like I'm sure he already is.

The paper began to shake so badly because the hands clutching it were shaking. I was furious to say the least. Here I was in the studio all the way in Brooklyn, busting my butt to make records and perfect my voice, and I had to read this foolishness. Instead of her just coming to me, or even waiting up on the couch for me to ask how my night was or why I was out so late, she just assumed the worst with a bunch of insinuations and religious talk. It was too much.

Just one letter from my mother could either make or break my day—or my spirit. It became really hard for me to speak to my mom at all. The frustration finally built up and took its toll. Since my voice was the only one that seemed to be permeating the walls, I found it getting louder and louder to the point where I found myself yelling at my mother.

There was this really bad argument we had over a letter she had written me. I came downstairs to my father fuming.

"Dad, talk to your wife. I'm tired of these f—ing letters!" I angrily waved the letter in his face. "She's driving me crazy." I was about seventeen or eighteen years old. Between puberty and just flat out being a bitchy teenager, I was tired. I was tired of feeling like she was always picking on me. Bullies at school weren't an issue; I felt like I was being punked in my own house.

"Mommy, calm down." The nickname Mommy is not like the Latino word, *Mami*. It's a Jamaican thing. He got up from his chair. He had been watching one of his favorite Western movies. He grabbed the remote to shut off the TV and focus his attention on me and all my frustration. "It's going to be fine, but Mommy, you've got to tone it down." My dad could have really let me have it for being so disrespectful, but instead, he gave me what I really needed, which was a listening ear. He could see it in my eyes that I was just so broken. He chose not to break me down any further, but to just hear me out. He knew I was pissed off, because I never cursed in front of him, but he was like my best friend, so I was hoping he would let it slide.

"No, Dad, I can't take it anymore." I was still fuming. "I'm not a damn baby anymore!" I started to walk away from him and head back up the stairs.

My mom was just coming down the stairs. I was so furious that I pushed her out of my way as I charged past her. I don't know what I was thinking. It was like an out of body experience. That's just how much of a toll our relationship, or lack thereof, was taking on me. I instantly felt remorse and fear, because I didn't know if she was going to clock on me, throw holy water on me, or what. I didn't even look back to see the look on her face. I just wanted to get the heck away from her. I got to my room and slammed the door then flopped on the bed like a teenager who had just gotten her video game privileges taken away.

I was so heated at the time that I just wasn't thinking straight. Regret, guilt, and shame for how I had reacted to my mother immediately took over my being. My tears of anger quickly turned to tears of sadness. I was talking to myself, saying, "You know better. You shouldn't let it rub you the wrong way. She was just raised differently. She doesn't mean any harm. She just doesn't understand."

But I would learn how to be calmer and wiser as I got older. Back then I was just trying to hold it together. I remember I always said this one particular comment to her, and she used to think I was joking: "You are lucky I am such a confident person, because if it was anybody else reading your letters, they would have jumped by now." But I was dead-ass serious.

All night I just tossed and turned. This was the worst confrontation my mom and I had ever had. It was to the point where my dad couldn't even calm me down. Usually my father's concern and attention, or even sarcasm for the situation, could cure any problem I was having. But that letter had just set me off to another level. It wasn't so much the content in the letter that had me angry; it was just the whole idea that my mother couldn't have a normal heart-to-heart, mother-and-daughter conversation with me. What was wrong with me? Why could the rest of the world, including other people's mothers, find it so easy to have a conversation with me, but my own mom couldn't? I just couldn't take it anymore. Still, she was my mother, and a level of respect had been crossed. I couldn't just let that go.

So, the next day I wrote her an apology letter and put it on her bed so she would see it when she came home from work. I wish I could have sat her down and told her the things I'd put in the letter. We hadn't really talked things out during my teenage years, so I have no clue how the conversation would have gone.

Call it bad communication if you want, but back then I thought communication took two people, and since I was the only one doing the talking, at that point in time, I didn't care if it was loud or not. At least someone's voice was going to be heard.

In spite of it all, my mom was and still is a great mother. She just had a way of communicating with me at times that wasn't good for a young girl coming up in Queens, New York. I wanted her guidance. Sometimes I just needed to hear her words, good or bad. Don't get me wrong; it's not as if no words were ever spoken between my mother and me—not like you could hear a pin drop in our home. That most definitely wasn't the case. We had family dinner every night, and sat and watched television and joked and laughed. My mom and I prayed together on the regular, and did the normal mother-daughter shopping trips. And you best believe if I was about to step foot out of that house, my mother was quick to lift her voice to find out where I was going and who I was going to be with.

"I'm just going over to Lauren's house." I'd pout with one foot out the door while my mother drilled me.

"Be back by nine, and make sure you leave Lauren's dad's phone number before you go."

I'd come stomping back in the house to obey my mother's orders. That's why I had no idea where all that crazy business in that letter about me being at the studio was coming from. Why not show the same type of concern verbally, as she had when I was going to hang out with Lauren? I guess with nobody's parent's phone number to give her, she had to trust me—well, me and Cousin Paul. Hmmm, perhaps that had been the real problem.

As bananas as it might have driven me, I actually look back and laugh sometimes when I think about my relationship with my mother. The conversations we never had. The letters we wrote. Yes, I said *we*. Heck, if you can't beat 'em, you join 'em. I ended up having to write letters back at times, because written communication was better than no communication at all. Some teenage girls would have been so lucky to even get that. Plus, in all actuality, who knew I'd grow up to be a song writer, sharing my deepest emotions and thoughts with the world? Truly, when it comes to that, it's second nature for me. I guess I have my mother to thank for that.

My relationship with my dad was just the opposite. I'm such a daddy's girl. My dad was more on the strict side because I was his baby girl. He was always firm in his tone, but never laid a finger on me. You know, one of those strict dads that when he spoke, I immediately sat my little ass still and paid attention.

My dad was very protective over his family. Here's an example: Last year, over dinner with a family friend, one of my girlfriends began to share a story about how someone had threatened her life. Let me first say that she is married. So my father abruptly cut her off and asked, "Wait a minute. Does your husband know that this person threatened you?" with a confused look on his face.

"Yes. Yes, he does," she replied.

My father unfolded his hands, sat up straight in his seat, looked her in the eyes and said, "Do you know what would happen if someone threatened my wife? They wouldn't be here anymore to threaten anyone else."

I looked over at my dad, wanting to get up and wave my church rag at him! He said one of those statements that warranted me to get up and thank Jesus that my father loves my mom with all his damn heart! I told y'all my daddy don't play about his family. He's a protector and a provider, period!

All I could do was just look over at my girlfriend and say, "Hallelujah."

And you want to talk about communicating? Tuh! My dad had absolutely no problem when it came to that. My dad loved to talk. Sometimes I had to stop him, like, "Okay, okay, I get it already. Sheesh!"

One night, back to my teenage years—I promise you seventeen got me in a lot of trouble—I stayed out past curfew. It was not too late, but late nonetheless. I had gone to the movies and dinner after school with a guy I was dating. My parents had the front porch light on for me, and they were both standing there waiting at the door. I scurried out of that green Acura so fast I don't think I even said bye to the boy.

I saw the look of fury on my father's face before I even got to the porch. As I opened the door, he wasted no time letting me know how he felt.

"Look, Mommy, do you realize what time it is? And you are out on a school night with a boy I do not know! Unacceptable," my father said to me sternly as I walked in the house. Even though he was using my endearing nickname, he still had all the bass in his voice. He was yelling; not to the point where I wanted to pee my pants, but just enough to remind me that I was the kid and they were the adults. "Boys are only going to want you because of your looks and what's between your legs. I know you are seventeen, but you can't stay out late like your brother does. He is a boy. There is a big difference."

See, I loved pulling that excuse out on my parents. "Why does Chris get to stay out whenever he wants? When he was my age, he would come home at midnight. What is the difference? It's not fair." One never knows what crazy person is out there waiting to catch a young girl by herself, but I was never by myself. That's why I always tried to make valid points. It was to no avail, of course, but at least I tried.

Even though my dad would shoot straight from the hip, I never felt like he was scolding me. Instead, I felt like he was giving me jewels of life. I looked up to my dad so much and valued everything and anything he told me. Those jewels were priceless!

In the conversations with my dad, he taught me how to be very vocal and very strong-minded. My dad's words gave me super powers. I'd walk away with my chest puffed for real. Boy, oh boy, did that turn me into a handful—and, might I add, a mouthful. Not only did I have my dad's mouth, but his temper as well. Man, when we get pushed to our limits, you better back the hell up. I would say whatever came to mind, whether it was rude or mean, and sometimes I didn't care how the other person perceived it.

I remember talking to Libbe, my brother's girlfriend at the time, and telling her straight up that she was a fool for staying with my brother. Now, family is family, so I would never rat on my brother, but I always gave her little pieces of advice that she never took heed to.

See, Libbe started to complain about my brother entirely too much. They were together for a total of about ten years. Yes, I said ten. I knew she wanted to get married, but my brother wasn't ready for what she was.

She also had suspicions of him cheating during the latter years, but she still stayed. Libbe was way too passive, and, brother or not, I don't want to see any woman getting taken advantage of. My brother knew she wasn't going anywhere, so he was not in a rush to fulfill all the desires Libbe wanted at that time. Libbe didn't demand the respect she wanted either. I always say men will treat you the way you allow them to. It's a man's job to respect a woman, but it's a woman's job to give him something to respect!

Now, Libbe was no slouch. She was five foot seven, very slender, very fair-skinned with Nigerian and Russian heritage. What a mix, right? She looked like a model. She could have demanded what she wanted, and nine times out of ten gotten it, but she wasn't outspoken back then.

Although I was younger than she was, I was stronger. I didn't let people walk all over me or take advantage of me. I hadn't meant any harm. I was just trying to be honest—another thing my dad instilled in me.

"Keep in mind that I'm an Aquarius too," my dad said to me. "We have a tell-it-like-it-is attitude about everything."

My dad being the same zodiac sign as myself only made it worse. Try having the two of us in a room. Baby, that was something. I definitely got my strength and courage from my father. The brains and the beauty I get from my mom—especially the brains. My dad was smart, too, and super handsome, but my mom was book smart. I didn't start looking like my dad until my late teens. I did have his Elvis Presley slick black hair, though. Other people be lying when they say "I got Indian in my family," But I really do!

My daddy was absolutely a G back then, and he knew it. My mother was a school teacher in Jamaica for three years, so any chance she got, she was telling me to read a book, making sure my grammar was correct, and that I wasn't using too much slang.

"Ma, I ain't even got time to do that right now. I still gotta do my homework," I said to my mother when she asked if I had walked the puppy.

Now, the presumed response one might expect from my mother was, "Oh, yes the hell you do, and you're going to do that right now before you touch your homework. I don't know who you think you are talking to, little girl."

Right? LOL. Wrong!

My mother said all pleasantly, "It's no, I don't have time, and I have to do my homework." She shook her head. "Baby, you have got to practice speaking proper English, even if you are in the house." Then she said, "And you most certainly are going to walk that puppy right now. You wanted a dog; you take care of it."

So, I took my tail outside and walked that dayum dog! The mess Soca would get me into. She was my first pit-bull of many growing up, clearly my dog of choice.

My mom still does that stuff to me now. If I go to the house to check on her and I speak any type of slang, that woman is still on my neck.

"Wassup, ma? You ain't fi'nna put on no clothes? Ain't nobody got time for you to still be in yo' silk pajamas at noon." My cousin Jackie and I stay getting on my mom about her silk PJs and not being dressed in the middle of the day. She will walk around the house way past morning looking like Meryl Streep.

"It is, *You aren't going to get dressed?*" my mother corrected me. "Young lady, what did I tell you about all that slang? And don't say 'ain't.' The proper word is 'isn't.' Where are your manners? You are going to slip up in an interview and sound uneducated if you keep this up."

Lord Jesus, I could always count on my mom to correct me. "Go 'head, Lorna, wit' yo' bad self," I would shoot back, and yes, she hated when I said that too.

"It is, *With your bad self*," she would murmur. I just had to laugh. Got to love that woman.

She's probably the reason why I read the dictionary so much. I would be in class using the biggest words, trying to impress my teachers. I'm not even going to front. Even to this day I love to use big words and show off my vocabulary.

The showing off part probably goes back to traits of my father. Anywhere he goes, he is the life of the party—dancing, making drinks, telling jokes, talking politics—so folks can blame my wonderful, sarcastic, outgoing personality on my daddy.

One time, my dad showed all the way out, you hear me? It was about three years ago, for Cousin Jackie's company awards dinner. She was the team leader for a company named Global Trans. Jackie's dad and my dad are brothers. We were all out at this beautiful banquet hall, supporting Jackie. It was me, Libbe, my friend Duane, Jackie's daughter and boyfriend, along with her parents and my father. My mom never liked to go to late events, and this was taking place pretty well into the evening hours. Anybody who knows Lorna knows that she is in bed come 7 p.m.!

Now, this awards dinner was most certainly a big deal to us, because Jackie's parents had been separated for years and never came to the same events. We normally took one or the other. Once all the awards had been given out—Let me say my fabulous cousin won six awards that night—we all hit the dance floor. This meant turn-up time to my father. We had all been sipping on wine most of the night, but know that wasn't why this scene was so funny. There was a well-dressed man with dreads on the dance floor all night. He had been busting out moves on his dance partner for a good hour. He was acting like this was an episode of *Soul Train*. Well, when the DJ put on the soca/reggae music, it was time for my dad to step in, literally. Thank God Duane was videotaping, because my dad would have thought we were lying about the dance moves he put on those people that night.

"Yo, D," I yelled out to Duane to turn around and put the camera on my dad.

"Oh my God! Pops is wilding out. Show 'em how it's done, Daddy," Duane yelled out.

My dad had tapped the well-dressed dude with dreads on his shoulder and cut in on his date. My dad was going to work on that dance floor. The only thing that was missing was for my dad to do the half split. He was whining down to the ground and putting all the young men at this event to shame. You would have thought my dad popped a molly at the rate he was going.

The lady he was dancing with was cracking up the entire time. She ended up being a friend who used to work at the airport with him, so she knew my dad was a trip. Everyone in our corner was screaming out, "Go, Daddy! Go, Daddy, go!" Man, it was hilarious.

As if that wasn't enough, then here comes Soul Train boy trying to one up my dad. Y'all, this dude actually did do the half split! We all went crazy then bust out with laughter because the poor man was having trouble getting back up. When the guy finally got up, he went over to my dad and they gave each other a handshake. My dad was the life of the party, just like I said.

My parents both spoiled me, but being that I was "Daddy's little girl," all I had to do was ask my dad for something and it was done. He made it very difficult for any man that would ever try to step to me. I was used to being treated like royalty by my father, so the man I dated had to emulate that, period! There was no compromising in that area.

As long as my dad was around, not many dared to step to me, but there was this one guy in my sophomore year of high school who thought he could be the exception. He had the nerve to come by my house checking for me. It was still light out, but I never gave this boy my address. You had to be really special to get my address outta me. I don't just introduce my parents to any ole body.

"Who are you here to see, young man?" I heard my dad's booming Jamaican accent. I was in the house, but that didn't stop my father's voice from traveling to my ears.

I was super nervous. My dad pretty much knew all of my brother's friends, so if a young man that he didn't recognize was coming to the house, it only meant one thing: Unless he was collecting for the Sunday paper, he was more than likely checking for me. It was like my dad could smell him coming for me.

I ran to the front window to catch a glimpse of who my father was questioning. It was this boy from school I had just started talking to. Man, I was calling him all kinds of names in my head. How was he just going to come over unannounced and uninvited? Even though I hadn't extended the invitation to him, who was going to believe that? He could have at least shown up with flowers so my dad would think he was a decent boy. Strike one. You always have to make a good impression on someone's parents. Now he was making me look bad. I sat on pins and needles just waiting to see how he was going to dig himself out of this pit.

"I'm, uh, here to see, uh, Olivia?" the boy stammered.

"Oh, are you?" My dad gave him the evil-eye once over. I swear that boy swallowed so hard I think his Adam's apple went down too. "Well, hold on. Let me go get her."

My dad quickly turned around, and I closed the curtain just as quickly. He entered the house and marched right by me. I was confused since he'd just told the boy he was coming inside to get me. Before I could even question where my father was going, I heard a sound from his bedroom. It was a click followed by another click. That's when I looked up to see my dad storming back by me, but he wasn't alone. He had Olivia: long, skinny, black, shiny Olivia . . . and it wasn't me.

With my hand over my mouth in shock, I ran upstairs to my room to get a better view from the top. I pulled the curtain back from the open window. It felt like I was peeking in on something I wasn't supposed to see, but I wasn't going to miss this, and I wanted to be far away from my dad when he came back in, in case he wanted to question me next.

"Well, here she is, son." He proudly admired his gun. "Olivia. You did say you came to see Olivia, didn't you?" I heard my father say in a threatening voice. "And now that you've seen her, you won't be needing to come back and see her again, right?" My father tapped his shotgun.

"Uh, no, sir. I mean yes, sir. I mean right."

That relationship was over before it ever started as that poor boy nearly peed his pants getting away from my dad.

My dad was such a gangster. It's his fault to this day why I like good guys with a bit of bad boy in them. If a man can't protect me the way my father always did growing up, then I don't want him. I wouldn't be the same outspoken, confident woman I am today without my father. Every daughter needs a father figure in her life; someone she can look up to and aspire to find a man like him. Someone to be an example of a good man, good husband, and to build future fathers.

My father used to play the guitar and my mom sang, so it was only natural I would follow in their footsteps and latch on to something that had to do with music. How crazy is it that I sing and play the guitar? I am my parents' child.

I would sing my li'l heart out. Didn't anybody dare to try to tell me that I wasn't Brandy. Brandy's song "I Wanna Be Down" was hot at the time. I would rush to turn on *Video Music Box* with Ralph McDaniels to see her video when I got home from school. Brandy was absolutely one of the artists that influenced me musically. Besides Anita Baker, Brandy has always been my favorite R&B artist for as long as I can remember. I have such an old soul.

Between my dad, mom, and Brandy, by the time I was sixteen, I knew making music in the studio was my passion, was what I was called to do.

A teacher once asked me, "What are you passionate about?"

I looked off and thought for a moment. "Passion? Well, I like—"

"No, I didn't ask you what you liked, or even what you loved. I asked you what it is that you are passionate about. What do you do every day that you love so much it doesn't even feel like work? That if it was something you could do every day whether you got paid or not, you would do it?"

I didn't have to think anymore. I knew exactly what that thing was. "Music," I blurted without even a second thought. "Music and singing and performing. Basically anything related to music."

"Then that is what you should be doing. Set a goal involving your passion and then achieve it. Think back to when you were a child. What did you love the most?"

"Music," was still my answer. "Singing, performing, making people happy with my voice, with my words, with my songs." I shrugged. "But I was younger then and—"

"It doesn't matter how old you are. It's never too early and it's certainly never too late to get something started. Society makes you believe that if you didn't achieve *it* at a certain age, you can't do it anymore. Well, let me be the first to tell you, you can do whatever it is you please, as long as you focus on the goal at hand. Prove to yourself that you can do it. Conquer the unimaginable."

Those words lit a fire under me that has never gone out. That burning sensation to still, after all these years, continue to make people happy with my music is like an eternal flame within my being. I'm passionate about evoking a certain emotion in people with my words, then singing it to the best of my ability and helping them relive a special moment through song. Music is my passion, period. It's that blaze that just won't allow me to walk away until I've accomplished the goals that I set for myself . . . even if it means getting burned along the way.

Chapter 3

"You're so beautiful, my baby, but just know that those looks won't last forever," my mom always made a point to tell me.

I looked at her like she was insane before I was able to actually gather my words to respond. "God gave me these looks for a reason, so why would they go away?"

I was a slender, nice-looking teenager at the time. I mean, I wasn't so naïve as to think I wouldn't ever age, but why would my looks go away altogether?

Once I got a little older, I knew exactly what my mother's intentions were in telling me that. It became evident that people will do a lot for a person just because of their looks. And just like the typical teenage girl, I was indeed into my looks.

My older friend, Alexis—Lexi is what I called her—taught me a lot of things about that fancy girl stuff: hair color, nails, handbags, etc. I had my own style, but I looked up to Alexis. In the mid-1990s, shaving your eyebrows and then drawing them back on was the in thing. I was all about that trend. Now, the verdict is still out on whether it was a good trend, but hey, I thought I was popping!

Hair color and styling was probably the most fascinating to me. I'd always worn my hair in its natural color, black, and down to the middle of my back. I can't even tell you how I started to get so sick of looking like and being called Pocahontas. At age fourteen or fifteen, I used to buy the hair color spray cans in brown or blonde and highlight a big chunk of my hair in the front. That was temporary and would fade within a few days. I needed to do something more permanent and less expensive. I was buying spray cans once a week. I knew just what to do and who to get to do it.

"Um, Lexi, you think we can color my hair tonight?" I asked in my li'l-sister, pretty-please tone one afternoon while we were in her basement watching videos.

"Sure, boo, but what color do you want to do?" she replied as she chewed on her gum as only a Queens girl does, making all those popping sounds. Alexis always had some darn gum!

"I don't know. Let's go to the store and look and see."

We threw on our shoes, grabbed our things, and hopped in her champagne-colored Honda Accord. Those were in then too. With the male singing group 112 blasting through the car radio speakers and all our windows down, we cruised past Linden Boulevard singing "Cupid." I remember us stopping at damn near every light, and talking with someone. Either Alexis knew somebody and we stopped to talk to them, or cuties kept pulling up to us trying to holla.

"Wassup, ladies?" one fella said out his window as they pulled up to us at the red light.

"Nothing, just chilling," Alexis replied as she chewed on her gum.

I tapped her leg and whispered, "Shorty cute." Alexis knew what I was thinking as she looked at me and nodded. They looked good for a movie and some dinner. The next thing I knew, we had their numbers and were back on our mission to the beauty supply store.

We must have gotten stopped like five more times. "Dag, li'l sis, I gotta keep an eye on you, 'cause these dudes are on you," Alexis said, giving me the wink.

"Well, you know I get it from my sister," I said, winking back at her.

Obviously this is when I started to learn that having good looks not only gets you material things, but it gets you lots of attention as well. We finally made it back to the crib so I could get my first hair-coloring session.

That one session turned into several, because I really liked the results of doing something different. First we started off with doing just blonde or brown streaks to see which colors I preferred. Before I knew it, we were doing full head colors of strawberry blond and burgundy. The first time Alexis did a red color on me, I thought the world was going to end.

"Stick your head in the sink," Alexis said.

"Okay, okay. I'm just trying to get a glimpse of the color, big head," I whined after trying to look at myself in the mirror on my way over to the sink, to no avail.

"Well, I don't need it looking like someone bled on my floor, so unless you're going to clean out this carpet, I suggest you be still and keep your *big* head down."

"Whatever," I said, sucking my teeth. I did as I was told and stuck my head in the sink, face down, for Alexis to rinse the color. I watched the red coloring go down the drain, but then I started to see something else going down the drain too. "Is that my hair?" I asked in a panic. "Why is there hair coming out? Am I bald?" I immediately reached for my hair to feel around.

"Girl, no, you ain't bald," she said as if she had an attitude that I'd even asked such a thing.

"Well, did the color at least take? What does it look like?" I kept asking question after question, but now all of a sudden the cat had Alexis's tongue and she wasn't doing any talking. "What? Oh my God, say something, big head."

Alexis still didn't say a word, but she did start laughing her head off.

"What? What is so damn funny?" I was getting heated.

"Relax, chica. I'm just ignoring you. I figured if I gave you the silent treatment then maybe you'd catch on and be silent your damn self," she said while laughing. "There is nothing wrong. It looks great. A little hair is supposed to come out, 'cause I stripped your hair."

Between all that laughing she was doing, girlfriend was not sounding too convincing. I couldn't wait to look in the mirror. Once she finished rinsing my hair, I tried again to make my way to the mirror.

"Uh-uh. You have to wait to see the finished look," Alexis insisted.

I just knew something wasn't right. I could feel it. Otherwise why wouldn't this girl just let me see my hair?

For the next hour I broke a sweat waiting—and the sweat wasn't from the hairdryer I was sitting under either. I was so nervous I was sweating bullets. I just knew I was going to have this Strawberry Shortcake–looking hairdo with bald patches here and there.

Once my hair was dry, Alexis commenced to flat ironing it. Almost an hour later, it was a wrap.

"Boom!" she said, pulling the towel from around my neck.

By this time, I'd been sitting so long that my legs were asleep. I could barely move.

"Before you had ants in your pants and could hardly sit still," she said, throwing one hand on her hip while pointing at me and twirling the other one. "Now you're sitting here like dead weight." She playfully pushed my shoulder. "Girl, get on up out of that chair and go see your hair in that mirror. You know darn well you're dying to."

I shook the numbness out of my legs, stood, balanced myself, and walked over to the mirror. I felt like I was walking the Green Mile. I just knew I was about to die after seeing what this girl had done to my hair.

Once I got to the mirror I still didn't look up at myself. I was looking down . . . praying. *Well, here it goes*, I thought, taking a long and deep breath. Then I did it. I looked up at the reflection in the mirror.

"Oh my God!" I screamed out as I began to pat my hair.

"Mm-hmm. I knew you'd love it," Alexis said, tooting her own horn after seeing the huge smile on my face.

And she was right. I absolutely did love it. This was her best work yet. It was no surprise that she was one of the baddest stylists on Linden Boulevard, where she worked in a unisex salon called How We Do.

"I do love it," I assured her again. "But you had me scared there for a minute. I thought I was going to have to deal with people calling me Ronald McDonald or invest in some good-ass wigs for a while." We both let out a laugh.

Alexis looked at me with a smirk. "You didn't think I was gon' jack my li'l sis up, did you? Damn, give a girl some credit."

The next day at school, mostly everybody was sweating my hair. I personally felt like my hair was fresh to death, but teenagers' opinions could be so darn harsh. This would be the first time I had done such a drastic color, but I was known for my hair color and styles, so I knew this could either go really good or really bad.

"Oh my God, what color is that?"

"Oh, girl, how did your hair not fall out with all that color? Don't you have a perm?"

"What products did you use?"

"She must be mixed with something, 'cause her hair is fresh."

I must admit, I ate up all that attention. My hairstyles and clothing started to become a big thing for me. I'd started something, so I had to keep it up. I remember in middle school I did this hairstyle that basically looked like a tree of circles on my head. I would put my hair in a high ponytail and stack my hair in pin curls, one on top of the other. I would then coat them with hairspray so they stayed in place all day. That was one of my signature hairstyles.

I always had to look the part, and in doing so, more times than not I managed to get what I wanted. There was this twenty-one-year-old guy I was dating when I was seventeen, and he spoiled me rotten. All he ever used to say was, "You are so gorgeous. You deserve diamonds." All he ever did was dote on my looks.

One day, we were out together and he took me to a mall in New Jersey.

"Look, babe. I'll be right back. I just gotta go pick up something real quick."

I was stunned. "Hold up. How you gon' take a doll to the mall but leave her sitting out in the car? Something is wrong with this picture."

His lips parted into a smile. "Trust me, love. I got this. I won't be long. You won't even miss me. " He got out of the car and did a light jog into the mall.

I was just sitting there watching him disappear behind the doors thinking, *WTF?*

In about fifteen minutes he was back out and joining me in the car.

Once he was settled, he turned and faced me. "This is just because."

I looked down to see that he was holding a little black box with a silver bow around it. "Awwww," I cooed, taking the box and pulling the bow off. I opened it up and there was the most beautiful set of diamond hoops I had ever seen. They looked like something a grown woman would own. As a matter of fact, I still have them to this day and wear them when I'm getting my classy grown woman on.

Not only did I get nice gifts, but guys used to send flowers to the house for me as well. My mom used to say, "Another bouquet for my little flower."

I think she loved the flowers more than I did, so I always placed them in her room or in the living room for her to admire. Almost every girl loves getting flowers, especially when they're young and impressionable. It seems so romantic, like a fairytale. Back then, New York boys knew how to get a chick's attention.

Guys in any borough knew all the pretty girls came from Queens. Ask LL Cool J and A Tribe Called Quest. They always rapped about Queens girls! So, that's usually the pickup line guys used with me: "You must be from Queens, pretty girl." Then there was the famous, "Do you have a quarter? My mom told me to call her when an angel fell from heaven." Then, of course, there was the worst one yet: "You know your alphabets? 'Cause all I see are U and I." OMG, were they serious? I was not impressed by those cornball lines, but me and my girls did think it was kind of cute back then.

Young Olivia's train of thought was on something else. I didn't crave or have to act out for attention, because I always just seemed to get it. I expected it. I'm glad that as I got older, I realized a doll should want quality over quantity. Took me a minute to get to that point, though, because what girl doesn't want a hundred men throwing themselves at her feet?

I didn't put myself out there like some chicken head, though, to get guys to do things for me just because. I really had to have some kind of interest in the dude. Plus, I wasn't thirsty. I was always picky, and I had my brother and his friends to emulate. I saw how they rolled. I was fortunate enough to have people around me who always wanted to do for me because they genuinely cared about and loved me. I was also fortunate enough to have never encountered an asshole in the young guys I dated as well. That happened later! Any guy I ever talked to or dated coming up was a gentleman. They knew how to treat a lady.

I was also fortunate enough to not have known that quote most females throw around: "All men are dogs" or "All men cheat." We all cheat for one reason or another, but as you grow you learn. Not all men cheat. Not all men are assholes. Not all men play games. You attract what you put out. Now, sometimes you may attract a dirt bag or two, but the issue is that some people don't know when to throw them back in the lake and hook a new fish.

It could be considered a gift and a curse to grow up and never know what it meant to not have the things I wanted. My parents spoiled me, my friends spoiled me, and my family spoiled me. I just thought this was how life was supposed to be. Besides, it wasn't like I just sat back and took, never giving. My family and the people I tended to surround myself with, like myself, were all giving individuals. I thought it was human nature to be that way, and therefore that it would always be give and take in life. I could not have been more wrong.

I encountered a friend or two that I had to cut off because of jealousy, or because I felt like I was being used. One girlfriend of mine, Kiesha, always magically appeared when it was time to go to a basketball game or some other star-studded event.

My best friend, Jade, pointed it out one day. "Do you notice Kiesha only wants to be around for the fancy shit or when the ball players are out?"

I honestly hadn't really thought about it. So, I took a minute and sat back to really think about the occasions Kiesha came around, and I realized Jade was right.

"All up in dudes' faces," Jade added.

I eventually just stopped connecting with Kiesha altogether. I kicked her and her ulterior motives to the curb. Who doesn't want to sit courtside? But damn—at least act like you care about me and not my floor seats.

I had another friend who just envied my career and fame. People think I'm closed off, but I definitely have my reasons. I let people in and they do dumb shit that makes me never want to see or speak to them again. I thought this one guy was a really good friend. He was like a brother to me. He didn't have a career, so he was just trying to get in where he fit in. He was around for years, but he was always a hater. Who knew he had hatred for me on the low? I'm not even going to mention that diva creep by name. He's lucky I'm even alluding to his ass. I wish I would give him any more shine.

When I caught on to his fuckery, I cut him off too, and told everyone he reached out to, to do the same. Let him be mad. I forgave him in my heart already, but I would never let him back in. Crazy thing is I still pray for him and people like him.

The funny thing about prayer: Prayer will make you apologize even when you thought you were right. It will make you humble yourself. Prayer will make you change from the inside out. "Lord, if you don't change the situation, please change me."

I had to change my way of thinking. Not everyone is going to be as fair and as good a person as I am. Not everyone is going to wish you well. Instead of getting mad and bitter and playing dirty like they do, I continue to be the bigger and better person. Now, I'm not saying that makes me better than they are, but it sure makes me different. Wink-wink!

God said forgive, for they know not what they do. I always say, "If I cut you off, it's probably because you handed me the scissors." Like Diddy said: "NO BIT-CHASSNESS PLS!"

It may take me a minute, but thank God for opening my eyes to wolves in sheep's clothing. Who needs fake friends?

When I had money in my pocket, I would buy my real friends things in a heartbeat. As a child, my dad would give me a weekly allowance. My mom always bought me clothes, food, and made sure I had money to get my hair done every week, so my allowance was mad money. Even though they supplied me with everything, I wanted to be independent. Folks might try to call me a lot of names, but one thing they will never be able to label me is a gold digger. I took my tail out into the world to find a job so I could buy things on my own. It always felt good to do for myself and not depend on anyone if I didn't need to.

The very first job I ever had was at BBH (Brown Brothers Harriman). They were an investment/banking firm located in Jersey City. One of my favorite aunts, Aunt Edna, who is my dad's sister, worked there.

"Auntie, if I give you my résumé, can you put in a good word for me at your job?" I asked her.

Being that I was also one of her favorites, I knew she would try to help. I gave her my résumé and she turned it in for me. Two weeks went by before I heard anything back, and when I did get news, I'm glad to say it was good news.

"Woo-hoo, I got it, Ma!" I said excitedly upon hanging up the phone with BBH human resources department. "I got the job!"

My mom rose to her feet and said, "Calm down, baby," with a pleasant smile on her face. "Where is it at?"

"Jersey," I sang, doing the happy dance, the one where I'm doing the Butterfly and snappin' my fingers.

"That's wonderful, baby, but how are you going to get there if it's all the way in Jersey?"

Now, I must admit, I hadn't even thought about that when I applied for the job, but I wasn't about to let that minor detail steal my joy. "Don't worry about all of that, Ma. I'm a big girl now," I said. "I can figure it all out. Besides, I am sure Aunt Edna will show me the way."

My aunt indeed took me out there one weekend, step by step, showing me how to catch each train and which stops I was getting on and off at.

Aunt Edna is still the best aunt ever. She was there for me my whole life. She had a huge house in Westbury, Long Island, and we all loved to gather at her house for special occasions. My auntie is and has always been fancy. No matter what time of the day it was, she had on her kitten heels and a pretty headband to match her outfits. She loved everything fur: fur on her shoes, fur hats. Man, I lost count of how many fur coats she has. When I was a kid and she used to babysit me, I would just watch her in all her glory. Now, a lady never tells her age, but Aunt Edna is still rocking her amazing furs and high heels, honey. Plus she rocks a mean red lip, and she is a fierce unnatural blonde like me!

At the time I got the job, I was on summer vacation from Hofstra University, where I attended for one year before transferring to Five Towns College. I worked there my entire junior year, and eventually they hired me full time. I learned about money marketing, business finance, how to build and set up major projects, and things of that nature. Aunt Edna had already worked there for years and thought it would be a great opportunity for me to learn and make money at the same time.

I was so hype because for one, I had never taken the train before or the Long Island Railroad, or as us New Yorkers say, the LIRR. And number two, I was getting paid nine hundred dollars a week! You know my bag game was ridiculous.

Even though I was eighteen years old and capable of getting to and from work on my own, my father always drove me to the train station every morning and picked me back up in the evenings. He had always chauffeured me, ever since I was in middle school, always looking out for his baby girl. I can count just a handful of times when I ever even had to take the bus.

My parents were always there to take care of me, so I made it a point to always take care of them in return. Whatever they needed, if I had it, they had it. On my payday, I loved to take them out to dinner and buy them nice things.

Just having that quality time to spend with both parents was something a lot of my friends didn't have the opportunity to do. Some of them came from single parent homes. They didn't get a chance to spend a lot of time with the one parent who did live in the home, because they were out working two and three jobs to keep a roof over their heads. So, time with my parents is something I never took for granted.

As I got older, I missed the days when I would come home from school and watch *The Cosby Show,* my favorite television show, with my dad. Of course, we would then have to watch his favorite show, *Jeopardy.* Then there were the times I'd make my mom watch *The Sound of Music* and *Sleeping Beauty* with me a thousand times over. Those little things with my family are times I look back on when I'm feeling alone. When I go visit my parents now, I still ask my mom to watch *The Sound of Music* with me.

Now, please believe me when I say times at the Longott household were not always like a scene from the Cosbys. There were times when I messed up. On one particular occasion, I messed up big time, but this chick is from Queens. I know how to get myself out of a bind by any means necessary. On this day, I thought I was in a scene from the movie *The Transporter.*

I had just recently asked my parents if I could change schools. I'd been going to Hofstra University, but because of my love for music I told my mom I wanted to go to Five Towns, where I could study anything that had to do with music 24/7. My brother graduated from Hofstra, so I think she expected us to be Bobbsey Twins and I would follow suit. It was bad enough we looked just alike, long hair and all, but did I really have to go to that school just because he did? I don't even like law. I was taking entertainment law because that was the closest program to music they had!

My parents bought me an I30 to kind of smooth things over and so that I would have a ride to the school I didn't want to go to in the first place. I admit, showing up at school with my own wheels was pretty cool and made it a little better, but remember, I was used to my parents giving me what I wanted. In this case, I hadn't gotten what I wanted, which was to go to a music school instead.

Well, one day after school I went to pick up Bingo.

"What's up, you little ounish?" I said to Bingo after he came out to the car.

"It's all good," he said, getting into the car with his bowl of cereal with strawberry milk. He always liked weird foods together—as if I should talk, Miss Peanut Butter and Jelly Sandwich with melted cheese on the side. Anyway, we were headed to Bundy's house to rehearse. I had my very first showcase coming up.

"Man, I do not feel like driving around the block," I told Bingo, realizing I needed to go back down the direction I had just come. With little contemplation, I threw that baby in reverse and was being this bad-ass, driving down the street backwards. Now, we all have been too lazy to make a U-turn or thought, *The street is too tight. I can just reverse.* The only difference with me is that I actually did it. I mean, Vin Diesel didn't have a thing on me, right?

The next thing I know, I slammed my whole right bumper into a parked car.

"Damn!" Bingo yelled. I looked over at him and saw that his cereal had gone flying all over his face.

I was stunned. "What am I supposed to do now?"

Without even thinking twice about it, Bingo said, "Floor it. Get the fuck outta here."

He did not have to tell me twice. I peeled off, probably leaving tire burns. At least this time I was rolling forward.

"I bet you my car is tore up," I said after we'd driven about ten blocks away. "What are my parents going to say? Mom is going to flip out."

"Pull over so we can check out the damage," Bingo said. "It might not be that bad. You might be able to hide it."

I pulled over and parked. Bingo and I got out and did a once over on the car. Everything was in perfect order, until we got around to that right side bumper.

"Yikes! I don't think we can cover that up," I said. The bumper was dented in, and it needed all new paint. The tail light was broken too. Touch up paint surely wasn't going to hide all the damage that had been done. We both looked at each other and just burst out laughing.

"Who the hell did you think you were, driving down the street backwards?" Bingo asked in between laughs.

"Oh my God," I said, bending over in hysterics. "I've got to go tell my parents. I can't hide this. They are going to kill me."

"Well, hell, you just almost killed you and me, so you must have a death wish anyway. Let's get the hell out of here," Bingo said, being all dramatic by climbing back into the car and putting on his seatbelt like it was a matter of life and death.

I pulled back off and headed to my house. I could hardly make it there without having another accident we were laughing so hard. Bingo would not stop cracking on me. By the time I pulled up at my house, I had to make myself stop laughing.

"Well, here it goes," I said, putting the car in park, shutting down the engine, and then getting out of the car. Bingo followed right behind me up to my door and into the house.

When I walked in and saw my mom and dad sitting in the living room watching television, my entire demeanor changed. Fear took over. The reality that they were about to wild out on my ass once I told them what happened hit me, and I immediately went into survival mode.

I don't know how I did it, but I managed to push a waterfall of tears out of my eyes. I started ranting, "See, that's why I said I didn't want to go to that stupid school. I knew something bad was going to happen," I cried.

"What the . . ." is all I heard coming from under Bingo's breath.

Both my parents jumped up to my side with horrified looks of concern on their faces.

"Livy, baby, what happened?" my dad asked me.

"They hit my car," I cried, pointing toward the outside where my car was parked. "I know somebody did it on purpose. They tore the back of my car up and just left it all messed up."

My dad immediately headed to the door with my mother on his heels.

I looked up at Bingo to make sure he was following suit. He had a look of complete shock on his face.

"What the . . . how the . . ." He was still speechless. "But you were just laughing your head off in the car, then you cried, and now laughing, and . . ." He looked like he was in the Twilight Zone.

I winked as I immediately mustered up more tears and went storming back out of the house in hysterics to meet my mom and dad at my car, where they were surveying the damage.

"Livy, honey, it's all right. We'll take care of it," my mom said.

And that they did. In a week, I had my car fixed back to perfect. The car might have been perfect, but like I said, I wasn't. To this day, Bingo said he knew I was born to be an actress after that incident.

Nonetheless, my parents loved them some me, and it goes without saying that I loved me some them. I remember sometimes after our little family nights we would often go to Friendly's restaurant, or my mom would take us shopping. She loved her some Macy's! I remember watching my mom try on clothes and just dreaming of the day I'd be able to shop for her and buy her something nice. With my mother's classy and fancy style in fashion, I'd sit there watching her twist and turn in the mirror, having no idea how I'd be able to afford to buy her such nice things, but that I'd make it my business to do so.

Chapter 4

I had this big showcase in New York City at this place that was known as the China Club back then. It was my first showcase for industry heads to see what I was all about. Cousin Paul had set it up. My cousin Paul was now my manager. It made sense, since he loved and believed in me, and my parents felt safe knowing he was with me at all times. Well, at least my dad knew I was safe. Mom was still worried about everything, thinking Cousin Paul was probably pimping me out to the fellas, but dad knew Paul had my back and wouldn't let anyone screw me over.

It was a packed house at my showcase. Even Jay-Z and Timbaland had come to check out the new artist who was going to be hitting the stage. I had already caught the attention of a few labels, including Arista, which Clive Davis headed.

The showcase had been on the calendar for a minute, but just a few weeks prior I'd already had a meeting set up with Keith Naftaly, who was the vice president at Arista records at the time. Clive Davis was setting up shop to open his new label, J Records. By this time I had a demo completed, because I had been working those long hours in the studio, despite the fact that my mom just thought I was playing around with boys. No, ol' girl was really up in that studio putting in her blood, sweat, and tears into an album. Tallest Tree Records, the company I had a production deal with, produced the majority of my music. They had a relationship with Keith Naftaly at Arista and got my demo in his hands. The next thing I knew, I had a meeting with this Keith guy.

I am grateful for my connection with Tallest Tree Records, because if it had not been for my initial connection with them, then the rest wouldn't have happened, but believe me when I say I was one hundred percent glad as hell when I severed my relationship with that company. Perhaps I shouldn't say everyone involved with Tallest Tree, but just Josh, the main perverted jerk that I had to deal with.

Josh lived in New Jersey with his wife and a three-year-old son that was just the cutest. At first, he seemed like he was all about business and ready to handle his business. Josh talked a real good game; it's just that the game he ultimately had in mind was one I wasn't willing to play. Alan, who was Josh's manager, had introduced us over the phone. We planned to meet Josh and his team of writers at his home, which had a built-in studio.

"Well, you know Josh has this amazing team of writers and producers in New Jersey that I really think you guys need to connect with," Alan told Paul and me. "Right now, they're doing a lot of work for some top artists. Come to the studio, meet 'em, check 'em out, hear what they do, and let's go from there."

It all sounded fair enough, so Paul and I set up a time to meet up with the team at Josh's studio.

"Hello, you must be Olivia," this fair-skinned Caribbean woman answered the door and said through this annoying, nasal, monotone voice. "I'm Mrs. Thompson, Josh's wife." She extended her hand. "So good to meet you. Alan says you're going to be a star." She looked at Paul. "Oh, nice to meet you too." She shook his hand and invited us into the house. "Everyone's down in the studio. It's right this way."

Paul and I looked at each other as we followed behind her, trying our best not to laugh. Was this lady for real with that voice? Thank God she was sweet though. Bless her heart, because God surely didn't bless that voice.

She took us through the living room and through the kitchen to the basement door, where we stopped and she knocked. She then looked back at us. "He keeps it closed when they're working." She smiled and then turned back around.

We smiled back, stifling laughter. I mean, she was the nicest thing ever, but again, that darn voice.

After knocking a second time, the door opened to Josh on the other side.

"Olivia," he said, his eyes lighting up like a Christmas tree. "You guys made it. So glad you could come."

Now, he was talking to both Paul and me, but he didn't take his eyes off of me once. At the moment, I wasn't really thinking anything of it because his wife was right here. I figured he was just being extra nice so that I'd ultimately decide to work with his team.

He took Paul and me downstairs to the basement, where there were three more guys working in the studio. One of those guys just happened to be the famous R&B singer Joe. Now, Paul knew Joe was one of my favorite male singers. Why did he not prepare me for this? Inside I was full of excitement and butterflies. I played it off, though. I went around and introduced myself to the guys, trying not to be too hype when I got around to Joe.

"Hey, Joe. I'm Olivia, such a huge fan of your voice," I said, smiling.

"Hey, love. Aw, thanks. Pleasure to meet you. Josh has been so excited to get us all together," Joe said

"Really?"

"Yeah. See, Joshua does a lot of my music too. He's a great producer."

Now, in my head I'm like, *Man, these guys are slick.* They had it all planned out. Have one of her favorite singers here and she's sure to want to join the team. Score one for the boys.

The guys played some stuff for us and ran lyrics by us. Paul and I were truly impressed. I watched as Joe and Joshua played the guitar together. And y'all know how much I love the guitar. They sounded amazeballs! Score two for the boys. They already had me hype with having one of the best male vocalists there, and on top of it, they had great music. Shiiiiiiiit, where do I sign up? LOL. That's what Alan had wanted us there for: to sign a production deal with them. Well, his plan worked.

So, now that I had this production deal I was in constant contact with Joshua and Alan. Josh was a really nice guy. Sure, he'd compliment me because I loved to work out and keep in shape. He even suggested some training techniques to me and bought me weights, a mat, and some workout clothes. Josh used to be a body builder, so I assumed he was just happy to be around someone else who enjoyed staying fit. He had won mad competitions and had posters of himself winning first place in several tournaments. So, I didn't find it strange that he had some interest in my working out and keeping it tight. In addition to that, I was a commodity. I was a product they were investing in, and in this business, looks matter—unfortunately sometimes more than talent. Thank God I'm equally blessed in both areas.

"Josh, you didn't have to buy me this stuff," I told him the day I showed up at the studio and he had it waiting there for me.

"I know, but I want you to get the full experience. I want you to be healthy so that you can produce better."

I raised an eyebrow. "Oh, so what you trying to say? I'm not producing up to par?" I joked.

"Oh, no. You are the best." He gave me a once over that was just a bit uncomfortable. "I bet you're the best at a lot of things. I mean, Olivia, you're just so beautiful. You're like this goddess."

Things were starting to get too weird for me, so I excused myself to go down and get started working with the guys. As I walked down the steps, it was one of those situations where I felt like his eyes were burning through my back, but I refused to turn around and look at him. Instead I just went and handled my business in the studio.

I continued to lay down tracks, and Josh continued to take care of me, making sure I had everything I needed. He always called to check up on me to make sure everything was good, but the phone calls became far more frequent than I was comfortable with. They were coming later at night, too, like I was dude's mistress or something.

"Hey, Olivia, it's Josh," he said through the phone. "Just calling to check in on you. I haven't seen you at the studio in a couple of days."

"Well, yeah, I had felt a cold coming on, and I didn't want to strain my voice."

"Oh, I'm sorry to hear that." He sounded most concerned. "I wish I was there to take care of you. If you were my woman, I'd definitely make sure I nursed you back to health all right."

I began choking. I couldn't believe he'd just said that to me. *Dude, you have a wife,* is what I was thinking.

"Oh, you don't sound good at all. Well, let me let you go. I'll see you in a couple days?" He sounded hopeful, like he was just missing me something awful.

"Yes," I replied.

"Good. Take care of yourself, and if you need anything, *anything*, Olivia, you know you can call me and I'll give it to you."

The call ended, but I'm sitting there staring at the phone like, *WTF?*

After that conversation, I made it a point to always have someone with me when I was at the studio. I was not going to be caught alone with that man.

One day we were all over at the studio putting in work, and Josh ordered some food. I excused myself to go upstairs to the kitchen, where the food was, and grab a quick bite. I was up in the kitchen when Josh came up and closed the basement door behind him.

"I'm hungry." He nodded at the food. "I came to get some."

He was looking hungry all right, but he was eyeing me instead of the food. He started walking toward the spread, but then passed it up and came in my direction.

"Whoa!" I put my hands up. "I don't know what you really came up here for, but it certainly is not for me."

My words did not halt his steps. As he came closer, I moved away. Within seconds, I was being chased around the table. For real—we were in a full-out cat and mouse chase. I'm looking like the poor Tweety Bird, and Sylvester the cat is Josh.

Dude was not playing around either. If he was ten years younger, he probably would have caught me, but I was a fast little whipper snapper! I hit them curves around that table like a pro, and managed to escape back into the basement. I immediately called Paul, told him what happened, and stayed on the phone with him the entire time while he drove to pick me up.

"I swear I am never coming back over here again," I told Paul as we drove away from the house.

Although I didn't spend as much time at the studio anymore, Josh would still call me like everything was everything.

"Hold on. Someone misses you and wants to talk to you," he said to me one night when he'd made one of his late night phone calls to me.

"Hi," this little three-year-old voice said through the phone.

I perked up immediately when I recognized it as Josh's son, Avery. I could just picture his pouty lips and gorgeous little face. "Hey, pumpkin. How are you?"

"Say *fine*." I could hear Josh coaching him in the background.

"Fine," the little boy replied.

I heard more mumbling from Josh in the background, and then the next words that came out of that child's mouth freaked me out to no ends.

"I love you, Mommy."

That fool was actually in the background, coaching his son into calling me his mommy. That was it for me. Shit got real, and I remained ghost. I'm glad the meeting with Keith was already set up, because I would have quit that production deal right there.

Later on, I asked Paul to get me out of that contract and get that company out of my life for good. It was way too stressful trying to deal with Josh and be political. Ain't nobody got time for that.

The day of my meeting with Keith in Manhattan, the outfit I wore was something else, or at least I thought it was. I had on a black-and-silver shiny halter top with a matching skirt. My mom had let me wear the only fur she owned at the time, which was a beautiful white/silver fur. I was fabulousness at its best! I had to walk in that building at least looking like money, since I was going to talk money.

As I followed Paul into the huge building, I just looked up in awe at everything. Tugging Paul's trench coat, I whispered, "This is where Whitney made her mark. Do you think they are going to like me?"

Paul turned and looked at me, and with a straight face said, "No."

I thought my heart was going to stop beating, but then a smile formed on his face.

"Are you kidding me, Mommy? They are going to love you. You are a star!"

Being the ball of emotions that I was, I started to feel the tears forming in my eyes. "All right, all right, cuz. I'm trying to keep it together here," I said, dabbing my eyes dry so as not to mess up my eye makeup. "You gon' have me looking like a raccoon."

"No, boo, we don't want that. You already looking like the bear from the Coca-Cola commercial is enough."

"Forget you," I said, play-punching him in the arm as we both laughed.

As we got on the elevator, my heart rate was pounding a hundred miles per hour. I felt all hot and nervous, as if I was getting ready to sing in front of a crowded room. But it was just one person I was going to have to impress for now. I just needed to go in there and wow good ol' Keith; then I knew Clive Davis would be the next person I needed to convince of my talent.

As the elevator doors opened, I took a huge, deep breath and stepped out. Up walks the sweetest, simplest looking man with ashy blonde hair, wearing a black turtleneck.

"Hey, you must be here to see me," he said with his huge, warm, positive smile. It was so contagious . . . and sincere.

"Then you must be the fabulous Keith I've been hearing so much about." I warmly smiled back. I could tell this man was genuinely happy to meet me. My courage level went up a couple notches.

Keith gave me a once over and said, "Well, you got all dressed up, didn't you?"

I acted as if this was my regular attire—and it kind of was. I dressed up a lot. Shoot, I used to wear ball gowns and my mom's white fur just to go to the movies with Libbe! He caught me on an off day.

I looked down at my fits. "Oh, I just pulled this together. You know, I wanted to make a statement," I said.

"Well, believe me, you sure did that." Keith smiled.

I wasn't sure whether that was good or bad at the time. Nonetheless, Keith took us into his office and we got right down to business.

"So, tell me, Olivia, where did you grow up? I'm told you've always loved to sing. Oh, and I hear you are in college right now?" He shot one question after the next.

"Well, I grew up in Queens, New York, but I was raised in Brooklyn and Jamaica. Not Jamaica, Queens. Jamaica the island." I always had to say that, because most people always thought I was referring to Jamaica right here in New York.

I stayed with my grandparents a lot in Jamaica. It's so different being raised on an island. The culture, food, and just the way of life is something one would have to experience for themselves to understand. Especially the food: ox tails, curry goat, rice and peas, escovitch fish, ackee and salt fish! Oh my goodness, how I wish I was in the Caribbean right now. Just the smell of my grandmother frying fish and dumpling could get me in the house.

My brother Chris and I would play with the farm animals in the backyard like they were pets. My grandmother had chickens and roosters and pigs. I remember one time Chris was in the backyard riding a pig. I don't know why he didn't just try to ride the dog. My brother used to do some funny stuff *back a yard*. All my Jamaicans know that means "back home." One time I tried to follow behind my brother and climb a tree. Let's just say I don't know how my knees aren't all scraped up from falling out.

Even though I was only about three years old, I remember it all. I went to school there as a toddler. Holy Childhood was the name of the school I attended. My grandpa always walked me to and from school. I really miss those days. My grandfather passed away a few years ago, and it was very hard for me. We would visit my grandparents almost every year in Jamaica up until I was about eighteen years old. Then I started going on my own whenever I could.

"Anyway, I am a music major," I continued telling Keith. "I attend Five Towns College in Long Island." By this time I had completed one year at Hofstra University and then transferred to Five Towns, where I could perfect my craft. "And all I want to do is sing," I cut to the chase.

He laughed at me and said, "Straight to the point, huh? I like that." He leaned back in his chair. "So, let me hear what you've got."

Now, I really wanted to tell him to turn around in that big swivel chair so he wouldn't be facing me. That was the shyness in me trying to take over. But I had to be a big girl and wear my big girl drawers, as some would say. If I was going to be a superstar, I couldn't be telling my whole audience of sixty thousand people to turn around while I sang. So, I took my mother's fur off and placed it down on the chair next to me, closed my eyes, and belted out "His Eye Is on the Sparrow."

When I finished and opened my eyes, Keith's mouth was wide open. Heck, a little sparrow could have actually flown in there.

"Wow!" was the word he managed to get out, and I was glad he'd managed to get it out before I turned blue. I'd been holding my breath, waiting on his reaction.

I let out a sigh of relief. Next, Paul suggested we play Keith some of the tracks from my demo with Josh, to give him an idea of what we were recording. I didn't have a particular sound at the time. I was just happy to have content.

After listening to three of the songs, Keith said he would talk to Clive Davis about me, and we'd have a follow-up meeting.

"Thank you so much, Keith, for this opportunity," I said as I stood and shook his hand.

"The pleasure was all mine," he replied then looked me up and down again. "Just tone down the outfit a bit when you meet Clive. It may be too much of a statement for him," he said and winked.

I just blushed and said, "I got it," before Paul and I exited his office.

When Paul and I got in the elevator, I was so darn happy. "Paul, did you hear that? We got a follow-up meeting with Clive! OMG. He liked me! He really liked me!" We grabbed each other's hands and jumped up and down in excitement.

After about two weeks of correspondence between Paul and Keith, they finally set up a follow-up for us to meet with Clive Davis. Keith had arranged for the transportation and everything.

"Well, here it goes, Daddy," I said to my father, who had been waiting with Paul and me for the car to show up. My mom was at work and my dad was on his way to work.

A black Town Car had just pulled up to my parents' house. I turned and looked my father in the eyes and gave him a kiss on the cheek. "This could be it." I gathered my things and told my father that I'd call him after the meeting. "Hopefully with some great news."

Paul and I eagerly jumped into the awaiting car. More nervous than before, I think I was quiet the entire car ride. About a half hour later, we pulled up to a beautiful building on Fifth Avenue. A doorman came over and helped us out of the car.

"Welcome," he greeted with a nod.

The doorman walked ahead of us and opened the door to the building, where another gentleman was waiting to show us into the penthouse. When the doors of the penthouse opened, I saw this big, beautiful spiral staircase that looked like it led straight up to heaven's pearly gates. I just looked at Paul and said, "I can't wait to live like this."

"Your time is coming, Mommy," he assured me with a pinch on the elbow. "Your time is coming."

We were escorted to the theater room, where Clive Davis and another executive were waiting for us.

"Hello, Mr. Davis. It is an honor to meet you," I said. I felt like someone had just introduced me to the President of the United States. Clive Davis was a music legend in my eyes.

"Please, call me Clive," he got up and said. "I have heard so much about you. I can't wait to hear you sing." He was very pleasant as well, just like Keith.

"And I can't wait to sing for you, Mr. Davis," I said as he sat back down and I remained standing.

Now, I heard him tell me I could call him Clive, but with my shot nerves and my mother's voice in the back of my mind saying to always address my elders accordingly, I still called him Mr. Davis for the duration of the meeting.

Always one to get straight to the point, without any extra talk, I belted out, once again, "His Eye Is on the Sparrow."

Clive was blown away. He gave me a standing ovation. "That was fantastic! I love it!"

Clive, like myself, wasn't the one to waste time with many words either, so after that, our little meeting was kind of brief. It wasn't like we sat around and had cocktails or anything. He thanked Paul and me for coming and told us we'd be hearing from him.

A few weeks later, one day I was coming in from class at Five Towns when my cell phone rang.

"Hey, Paulie," I answered after seeing his number on the caller ID.

"You's a bad motha, superstar!"

I nearly dropped the phone, because I knew he was going to give me some great news. There was far too much excitement in his voice for it to have been bad news. "What? What are you talking about, Paulie? And don't torture me over here, cuzo."

Then he simply said, "It's a done deal. They want to sign you, Mommy!"

"Holy shit!" I shouted through the phone receiver. I felt like I had been waiting forever to hear back from the label. Now I'd be waiting again, as Paul relayed to me that the next step was the label calling back to set up another meeting with Clive Davis.

A few days later the call came. We were invited to Clive's mansion in Westchester, where I was going to sign the paperwork to finalize my record deal. The deal I was about to sign was more than fair. I didn't think I would ever see that much money in my young age! And it was going into MY BANK ACCOUNT! Jackpot. Look at God. Back then we got production budgets, studio budgets, monthly living expenses, and an upfront advance. To say I was happy was an understatement.

All I kept thinking was how this was it. I was going to buy my parents everything they'd ever wanted—a new car, a new house even. I was going to get myself every Fendi bag ever made, save the world, feed the children . . . anything and everything. I was hype!

Once again, the record label had arranged transportation for me to get to the meeting, but this time it wasn't a Town Car. Imagine my excitement when I saw the shiny black limo coming down the block.

I had on white leather pants, a pink halter top, and my sheer pink Dior shades. I was ready for Hollywood, honey. My brother and parents walked Paul and me out the door like they were seeing me off to prom.

"Okay, we are good," I told everybody once we made it to the limo. My mother went to give me a hug. "No, no, Ma, don't hug me. You are going to mess up my hair," I said.

"Oh, you're a mess, Liv," Paul said.

"Knock 'em dead, Mommy," my dad said as he waved good-bye to me. "You got this."

The proud look in my parents' eyes became so overwhelming; I had to hurry up and get out of there before the waterworks started.

The limo driver opened the door for Paul and me, and we got settled in. The driver returned to the car and then off we went to Westchester. This was the longest drive ever. It took us about three hours to get there. As we got closer to Clive's compound, the homes got bigger and bigger. When we finally pulled up to Clive's estate, my whole jaw dropped.

Nudging Paul, I said, "Oh my God! Do you see this? It's frickin' insane!" Man, you couldn't even call something that size a house. It was breathtaking. He had a guest house next to his main house, and it was just as big as the main house.

I felt so nervous as I got out of the car, but my production company and some of Clive's staff were outside waiting to greet me. Familiar faces definitely helped to settle my nerves. It was like a scene right out of the movies. Everybody was standing out there looking all happy, and some people had drinks in their hand like it was a real red carpet celebration.

When I exited the limo, Ken Wilson and Ron Gillyard greeted me. They were A&Rs of the label. They introduced me to a few people outside before we all entered the house together. It felt like we were in the Hamptons somewhere. In my head I just kept saying, *This can't be real. This is just crazy.*

I walked in looking every which way but straight. The house defined fabulousness. It was as if Versace had furnished it himself. Custom glass tables and vases were everywhere. There were huge mirrors, furniture styles I'd never even seen before, and rooms upon rooms upon beautifully furnished rooms.

"Olivia, it's good to see you again." Clive greeted me with a hug. "Are you ready?"

Hugging him back so hard, like he was my fairy god-father, I replied, "Yes, Mr. Davis, I've been ready." After breaking from the hug I looked around. "By the way, this is a beautiful home you have."

"Why, thank you. Would you want to take a tour first before we get down to business?"

"Yes, of course." I grinned all big like the Grinch who stole Christmas.

He held out his left hand for me to put my arm in his and said, "Shall we?" as his extended right hand led the way.

We walked around by ourselves, and I think I was in shock that I was in a place that beautiful. That I was with the famous superstar maker, Clive Davis. That I was about to sign a record deal, yo! Inside I was screaming; on the outside I was so quiet. It wasn't until we came upon his wall of fame and I saw all the pictures of Whitney Houston and a few other singers hanging on the walls that I became truly overwhelmed. I just stood there staring at Whitney's picture, my eyes filling with tears.

"You know yours is going to be up there next, don't you?" he said, pointing.

I turned to him and said, "That would be the biggest honor ever. Mr. Davis, I am so excited. I have no words."

"Well, find your voice, because you are going to be needing it to sing your way into the world's heart, my little Whitney."

As badly as I wanted to cry, I managed to blink those tears away and keep it together.

We walked back into the living room, where everyone was waiting for us. That's when they brought the paperwork out for me to sign. I went over to one of the beautiful oval glass tables he had in the living room and kneeled down and asked everyone to pray with me before signing it. Everyone bowed their heads with me as I prayed. I then took a deep breath and signed on the dotted line.

It was so surreal, such a huge step and a big deal for me. Clive had all his top VPs at the house for this meeting. I felt like a million bucks . . . and that I was about to make a million bucks too!

We went into the label's office within the next two weeks to pick up my first check—my first check from a major record label deal that I had been dreaming about since I was eight years old! When I saw the amount on that check, I didn't know what to do with it.

Two hundred thousand dollars was my cut of the first advance. What the hell was a young nineteen-year-old girl supposed to do with all that money? I looked at that check for the rest of the day. Literally just looked at it and thanked God. I was so ecstatic to get this record deal, and I couldn't get over the fact that Clive Davis took pride in parading me around the office like the next best thing since sliced bread.

After signing me, several other acts were then signed to J. Records, including Busta Rhymes, Wyclef, Alicia Keys, Jimmy Cozier, and O-Town. My name would be mentioned in the same breath as theirs? Busta Rhymes and Wyclef were the first artists on the label that I was introduced to. Wyclef was so pleasant, and Busta, well, y'all know he was animated as hell. Busta will always be a ball of energy.

I was amongst the best in the business. This was crazy. All in one month I had signed my deal and was now being introduced to superstars in the business—not to mention the best stylist. Ron Gillyard hired June Ambrose and her team to find the best clothing that worked for my style. June was styling for Puffy at the time, so I knew she was A-1.

I met one of my close friends through June. One of her assistants at the time was a girl by the name of Sharrell Williams, a bright, friendly, and ambitious young lady. I took to her right off the bat. Something about her stood out. We have been friends for twelve years and counting.

Man, I remember having the best sleepovers at Sharrell's house. It didn't matter what time it was; if one of us needed the other, I was on the Belt Parkway headed to her, or she was on the Cross Island headed to me. We both had blond Yorkshire terriers at the time. Mine was Scooby, and hers was named Doo Wop. Those two were so darn feisty with each other, but they had no choice but to get along, because we were always together.

Sharrell, whom I nicknamed Shaya, made me the best salads. I was always over there late, so we called ourselves trying to be healthy when we got hungry. She would make me banging turkey spaghetti with garlic bread and a strawberry and mango salad. Y'all don't understand! I would live for one of Shaya's salads. Although we both became very busy in our separate careers, we were and still are always there for each other.

The next part of business was doing a promo tour and traveling. I got to be in cities and countries that I only saw on television, eating the finest foods and buying the best in clothes and shoes and technology. I was very much into video games back then, but the best part overall would have to be the free clothes.

I loved wearing sweats on the road because it was so comfortable to travel in. The first time I got a package from Sean John . . . Oh my gosh, the boxes were filled to the top, and it was never just one box. I should have been a female model for Sean John back then, because it's all I wore when I was traveling.

I had to pinch myself and make sure all of this was really happening. "You mean to tell me I don't have to buy clothes from these companies?" I remember asking when I received my first set of packages, after digging around for an invoice. "Designers are just going to send me free boxes of stuff every month?"

What I didn't know was that when you are a signed artist, especially to Clive Davis, designers want to see you in their clothes. They want other people to see you in their clothes for publicity. I still lived with my parents, so every time I would come home off the road from traveling, packages would be waiting for me at their house.

I thought I had died and gone to retail heaven! Clearly this lifestyle was not helping the fact that I was already spoiled. But again, I always gave. My motto was still, "If I had, my family and friends had." I would ask for doubles of everything, or ask if I could have them in different colors, and I would then turn around and give them to my peoples. Companies would send catalogues of their clothes to the office, I would just circle what I wanted, and the label would send it back. All I had to do was wait for the items to come in. Who knew?

What I would soon come to realize, though, was that sometimes it is not good to be handed things. You forget the purpose of working hard and achieving things on your own. In addition to that, no matter what it looks like, everything comes with a price.

Chapter 5

Home, sweet home! The BMG Building in New York City had now become my regular stomping grounds. As I walked into the building and checked in at the main lobby to go upstairs, my right hand, Paulie, was right there with me.

"So, how does it feel to be the first person signed to J Records, Mommy?" Paul asked.

I blushed and shook my head. "Clive Davis, cuz. I'm with Clive Davis!" I still had to pinch myself every so often to make sure I wasn't dreaming.

We got on the elevator and traveled up to the ninth floor. As the doors opened, a big sign greeted us that read: J records. I stepped off the elevator and noticed something else.

"Paul! Look!" I pointed. "There is a picture of me up already." I was sounding like a preschooler showing her parents her first drawing on the refrigerator. We'd done a photo shoot for some promotion, but I had no idea a picture of me would already be gracing the wall.

Everyone was equally excited to see me. I felt honored, privileged even, that I was the one chosen to flagship the label. The company wasn't even fully up and running. Offices weren't completely furnished, and people were just settling into their jobs. This was going to be a tough task, since mine would be the first project to go out.

In the months to come, we prepared to choose all the cuts for the album. One of my favorite songs that I wished was a single was titled "It's On Again." That song still makes me feel like I'm on a deserted island, just me and my boo with cherry blossoms blowing in the wind.

I had a lot of great records, but now that I think about it, the album really had no direction. Every record was different. You know how on *Project Runway* the designers who get to show their collection at New York Fashion Week have to have cohesive pieces? Well, let's just say my collection of songs lacked cohesiveness. At the time I didn't think about sequencing or how to make an album flow. I just wanted an album out.

The record label chose to go with the song "Bizounce" as my first single. I remember bickering with my production company about what my first single to drop should be. Yes, "Bizounce" was a good song. It had an upbeat tempo, which worked in the clubs, but it didn't reflect me as an artist. My friends Bingo, Corte, and I wrote "Bizounce" together, so it was definitely a favorite. I just wasn't feeling it as the song that would introduce me to the world.

We also had to work on the album photo shoot. The staff wanted me to be appealing. I had to have a certain look. I was supposed to be like the girl next door, but with a little sneaky devil on her shoulder. This one shoot we did for *Vibe,* for me, was so racy. I had on a waist-length silver-and-beige fur with the tiniest pair of shorts. I was sitting down, so it looked like I was only wearing the fur. My hands were folded to cover my private area. I looked like a total bad-ass, but man, was that shoot sexy.

I will never forget the first quote I saw from *Billboard* magazine in 2001: *"Newcomer Olivia has the mouth of a bad girl and the voice of an Angel."* I still have the plaque of the album cover that they wrote this on. I keep it hanging right up in my guest room, along with the rest of my plaques, so that I'm reminded every day of where I started. Not that I need a reminder, because a chick is still grinding and will always be. I'm a born hustler.

I did a huge amount of press, followed by shows and meet and greets. The meet and greets were settings where I would meet the fans up close and personal, sign autographs, and take pictures. In addition to that, I had all kinds of business meetings just to make sure everything was in order. I was on and off the road for months, and in and out of fancy hotel rooms with my cousin Paul still by my side. I didn't care about all the hard work. I enjoyed the grind if it meant one day I'd hear my songs on the radio. But even with all this hard work, I still managed to find the time to spend with my boyfriend, Neko Hassanali.

Neko lived on the other side of town. He was off Merrick Boulevard, close to where Bingo lived. As a matter of fact, it was Bingo who introduced us. When I wasn't handling music business, my friends knew to look for me at Bingo's or at the Hassanali's.

"Where's your big-head brother?" I asked Maria, Neko's fifteen-year-old sister, as I entered their house.

"I don't know. Somewhere." She'd removed her thumb from her mouth just long enough to get those words out. She then popped it back in her mouth like a little kid. With thumb in mouth, she turned and yelled, "Neko, Livy here!"

"What's all that yelling about?" Mrs. Hassanali came out of the kitchen dressed to the nines in her Sunday's best, with a stirring spoon in her hand.

I just loved Mrs. Hassanali. She was the sweetest, most God-fearing woman I had ever met at that time—besides my mom, obviously.

Neko's family was from Trinidad, so you know we ate well whenever I was there.

"Ma, please tell me you made roti and chicken with chick peas," I said.

She could hear the excitement in my voice. "Girl, I just got in from church, but you know I made your favorites. I was warming it," Mrs. Hassanali said in the most fly Trini accent ever. "You can eat whenever you're ready."

I knew she was going to have the kitchen working on overload, which is why that day I couldn't get over to their house fast enough. At this time, I had a silver Infiniti I30. It was kitted out with nineteen-inch rims, a goose neck TV in the front, and a mean custom Bose system. I know I had broken several traffic laws driving over there.

I could smell the curry and chick peas and potatoes with every step closer to the kitchen.

"Mmmm, feed me," I called out like Seymour in *Little Shop of Horrors*. The kitchen table had a spread of all my favorites: rice and peas, roti, curry goat, chicken and chick peas, and potatoes. My mouth was salivating.

Mrs. Hassanali had trailed behind me into the kitchen.

"Ma, you are too good to me," I said, turning and giving her a hug.

"Oh, just make your plate, li'l girl." She smirked at me. "No need to butter me up."

Neko walked into the kitchen with his curly, red-dish-brown hair in a ponytail and his cute dimples. He immediately laughed at me, because he knew I would greet the food first before I greeted him.

"Oh, shut it. You know I'm always hungry," I said to Neko while I fixed my plate. Once I'd loaded my plate, I sat down at the table and dug in. I cleaned my plate so fast it was a sin and a shame.

We all ended up in the living room just chilling, and then my cell phone rang.

"Gyal, tun on di radio. You deh pon Hot 97." It was cousin Jackie. "Hurry up, then call me back."

I dropped the phone and took off running like a derby horse, you hear me!

I ran to the radio in Neko's room, turned it on, and immediately started screaming. "Neko! Neko, baby, come here!"

Everybody heard me going off and had no idea what was going on, so Neko, his mom, and his sister came running into the room all at once. "What is it? What's going on? What's wrong?" They each hit me with questions all at once.

"Shhh," I said, placing my index finger on my lips. "Just listen."

The next few seconds no one spoke, until it hit everyone exactly what and who they were listening to.

"That's you, Olivia. That's you!" Neko shouted, ten times more excited than I was.

Within seconds, we were all screaming, shouting, hugging, and jumping up and down as "Bizounce" played on the radio. I felt like I had hit the lotto and these were the only people I had told, and now here we stood all celebrating together. It was a moment I will never forget.

After that realization that I was on my way to stardom, more hard work was to follow. I had to make sure dang near every song I put out got play. So of course, I was always bugging Paul to go to the J Records office with me whenever I was in New York. I wanted to stay on top of things. I wanted them to see that I was an artist ready to put in work.

"Come on, Paul. You were supposed to be here to scoop me already. You running late. Let's go check in with Ron and Ken at the office," I puffed through the phone receiver.

"You the one that's late, Mommy," Paul said. "I'm right outside."

I hurried to look out the window as if he was lying. There he sat, waving sarcastically at me through the window. "OMG, jerky. Why didn't you say something?

I'm coming down." I hurried out to Paul's car so we could be on our way.

Our car rides to the label were always the best. Paul and I always told jokes, and we had the best family bond. We got to the label, and as always I was my happy self, bouncing in and out of offices, greeting everyone, showing love and getting mad love in return. It truly felt like home and that I was amongst my second family. If there was a new face around that I didn't know, I would walk right up to them and introduce myself.

"Hey, Daina Dane." I greeted one of Ron Gillyard's assistants as I peeked my head into her office.

"Hey, boo. We've missed you. What's been going on?" she asked me.

I walked in and took a seat while Paul went and chatted it up with someone else. Daina and I went on and on about life on the road. Next, I paid Ron's other right hand, Ampora, a visit. I just adored Ampora and Daina, but Ampora, who I nicknamed Po, and I were like besties in high school. When the two of us got together, it was one of those "Ooh, girl, I gotta shut the door and fill you in on the tea, honey," type of stories being swapped.

Ron hated it, because he knew we were always up to no good. Ron was assigned head A&R over my project. Now, I would have considered my relationship with Ron a great one. I mean, he always looked out for me and gave me advice. He was one of those guys who I felt would always help steer me in the right direction. So, when Paul dropped the bomb on me that he heard through the grapevine I was going to be released from the label, I was furious and confused. Surely Ron would have told me if something like that was in the works.

What I didn't know was that some people were going back to the label telling them I wasn't happy. Paul tried to find out as much inside stuff as he could and bring it back to me. I had absolutely no idea any of this stuff was going on or why anyone was trying to throw me under the bus. The shade, honey. I never really got the full story to this day—just rumors, stories, hearsay, and gossip.

I was too depressed and pissed off to even go to Clive. He was the big man on campus. What would I look like taking this drama to him? I thought I'd look like a diva who didn't even have a record out yet and was already causing trouble, but I was really just a concerned artist trying to figure out what was up. Instead, I sat on my hands, bit my tongue, and allowed Paul to be my voice and handle all the questioning. That is what having a manager is for, so I just let him be a manager.

Unfortunately, Paul was coming up empty on answers. "Nobody has had anything bad to say about you, Mommy," Paul relayed. He was just as baffled as me about the whole situation.

It was like this entire situation was a mystery on both sides. I just couldn't wrap my brain around it, and neither could Paul.

"Paul, I'm confused. Am I missing something?" I said on a ride back from the office. "Do you think it's because I didn't take that one phone interview while I was overseas? That time I was sick?" I questioned. "Hell, I was sick as a dog. I had done press all day and had just gotten back into the hotel room. I was in bed and under the covers when that interviewer guy called."

"I told them that you were exhausted and wasn't feeling well; that I would relay any messages, interview questions, et cetera," Paul reasoned. "They declined the offer, so what else could we do?"

I thought for a moment. "Oh my God! Do you think the reporter I turned down was that important? Who was he with? Do you remember? What if it was something the label had set up and then he went back and told them I was a bitch or something?" I threw my hand on my forehead. "Damn it! Why didn't I just take the call? But we told him to please reschedule it for another time. I remember you distinctly saying that, Paul."

I'm sure Paul thought I was being a drama queen, but this was my life—my career. "I'm sure it's all a misunderstanding," he said.

"Well, I can't rest until I get to the bottom of this."

"Well, whatever happens, you know I got you," Paul assured me. "I'll always have your back."

I believed Paul and I trusted him to always have my back, but first I had to figure out who'd stuck the knife in it. I went through this entire period of trying to figure out what had gone wrong with my relationship with J Records. No one had a real answer for me—and I mean NO ONE! So I started blaming myself and nitpicking at myself, trying to figure out what I might have done to have brought this on myself. Did they just not like me anymore? Did I piss off the wrong person? I mean, I was only twenty years old. I was going to make mistakes, but they didn't have to drop the kid.

It felt like my dream was beginning to slip from my grasp. I'd wanted this so badly, and I'd always gotten what I wanted, so this could not be happening—not to me. Clive Davis absolutely adored me, and I felt the same about him. What happened to all the excitement of signing me and how ecstatic people were to work on my project?

I was really hurt and in pure confusion when all of this happened. I cried once or twice by myself. Nobody, not even Paul, knew that. I always had to be strong and hold it together in front of others. I was the foundation of my future. If I cracked and caved in, then everyone else around me surely would as well. We had to be strong and work through this somehow.

I had always been a hustler, so one day I just pulled myself together and gave myself a pep talk. "I'm just gon' push forward. You are still super young and a star. You can get another deal easy!" I brushed myself off, said my prayers, and put one foot in front of the other on the path toward my destination, not knowing how far the journey would be, or what might sidetrack me along the way.

Chapter 6

The whole ordeal with being let go from J Records was devastating. Because I hadn't yet learned "The Politics in the Building," I had been in the dark, clueless to the fact that this was all just a strategic setup. Little did I know at the time that the plan was for me to go over to Interscope Records with one of the executives from J Records, Ron Gillyard. See, Ron had gotten a VP position at Interscope but kept it on the low while we were at J Records.

"Listen, Liv, you are going to be good. I'm going to take you with me when I leave," Ron assured me. "Just relax and follow my lead." Ron sounded both convincing and confident.

"Are you sure? How is that going to work? I mean, if I'm not wanted, I'm not wanted."

"It's not about you not being wanted; it's about where you are wanted. I have a very high position at the new label, and I can bring who I want, so you are going to be my first signee."

Oh, goodness. Here I was about to be "the first" again. After how it worked out that last time, I can't say that I was jumping up and down. Some worry and concern weighed me down a bit, but still I was relieved to find that I wasn't just being left out in the cold.

"All right, Ron. I trust you on this one. Just be sure of what you are doing because my blood pressure can't take any more of these surprises, and I ain't even got high blood pressure. Y'all killing me here."

"Trust me, Olivia, no worries. Ron here is going to take great care of you."

I wanted to see my dream through, but at the same time I just wanted all the confusion to be over so I could get back to making music. Ron promised me things would be better at Interscope, and seemingly they were.

Jimmy Iovine was the president of Interscope Records. He was mostly known for bringing in Eminem and Dr. Dre. My first meeting with Jimmy Iovine was so fast and to the point that if I blinked I would have missed him say, "Well, sign the girl. What the hell are you waiting for?"

I guess Ron really had everything set up.

Chris Lighty was in the meeting with us. Paul wasn't in attendance because, I assume, he trusted Ron to have everything under control. Ron brought Chris in because he thought Chris could help manage my career. By this time I was about twenty-two or twenty-three and still learning a lot.

Again, this meeting really was a blur. I don't remember much. We didn't go into any detail; just that we would hash everything out on paper. Jimmy Iovine just wanted to meet me in person. They told me I would have to relocate to Los Angeles, where the main Interscope building was. Ron told me he would make sure my living arrangements were all taken care of.

After that meeting I said to Ron, "Man, if I would have known it was going to be that easy, I would have asked for a new car too." I mean, it seemed like things were only going to change for the better, and what wasn't changing were things I actually preferred to stay the same. For example, Paul being my manager. But this is where that tricky word "politics" once again came into play.

I had Paul as my manager when I was with J Records and then brought him with me over to Interscope as well. Because of all the politics going on, he thought it would be good to have someone co-manage with him, in order to have my project run smoother. Paul was just looking out for me, trying to make sure I had an insider, so that both my back and front were being watched at all times.

This wasn't some grand idea Paul had come up with on his own, though. Ron had dropped the bug in Paul's ear, telling him he thought it might be a good idea to have Chris on my management team, since he had been in the game with numerous artists under his belt. Paul and I went for it, but it turns out that it wasn't the best move for Paul. He ended up, slowly but surely, letting the new company, Violator Management—which Chris headed—push him aside and handle everything themselves, even my day to day business, simple stuff like connecting phone interviews or coordinating photo shoots, letting me know what packages had arrived at the office for me.

Paul half knew what was going on with my career, and I can't say he showed the greatest interest anyhow. So, here I was in the middle of trying to deal with a new label, new management, and a whole bunch more unnecessary politics. Things started to get messy. I felt like I was going to have to choose between my new management company and current manager.

I was so torn. Paul had helped raise me. He was the one who made sure I got back and forth to the studio back in the day when I was trying to land a record deal, so to basically see him throw his privileges away like that was very disturbing. I had to call him out on it.

"Why don't you go up there and ask Chris what's going on? To keep you in the loop?" I had urged Paul. "I mean, you rarely come to meetings, and you've never came to any of our show dates." I threw my hands up in the air. Paul couldn't get a word in edgewise. I was so frustrated with how things were going down management-wise. "Jesus, we performed at Jones Beach and Hot 97's big summer jam this year, both huge events that you did not bother to come to. I feel like you are not even supporting me anymore."

Paul didn't book any gigs, but as co-manager, he still should have been showing his face. Violator Management took care of all my bookings and showed up to make sure everything was in order. At the end of the day, though, they still had to split the twenty-percent management cut with Paul. How long did Paul think Violator Management was really going to let that go on?

"Well, I feel like y'all pushing me out," Paul replied defensively.

"I'm not pushing you out. You're doing that to yourself."

I hated to admit it, but I could see how they could have easily moved Paul to the side. The most Paul did was call up to the office every once in a while. I felt like, well, if he didn't care how they treated him because of his complacent attitude, then why should I? I felt like he had gotten far too comfortable without putting in the necessary work. He seemed to have had this air about him, this attitude like no one could knock him out of his seat. They were clearly setting up camp without him, yet he still seemed to think he was in control. How the hell do you think you still have control if these people don't see nor hear from you? As far as they were concerned, they were doing all the work. Paul exed himself out and made it easier for them to storm the castle.

That situation definitely helped shape me in the industry. I vowed to never let anyone take my spot or push me out of a position that I had rightfully earned.

Although getting dropped from J Records had put a damper on things, now being over at one of the most respectable labels in the game, Interscope, I was so happy! I had moved to Los Angeles and loved the change of scenery. Imagine if I had allowed my release from J

Libbe, my brother's girl for 10 years, is still my best friend.

Doing my "tah-dah!" pose

Dad and I in Aruba

Celebrating my birthday

Mom with me and my brother

Dad

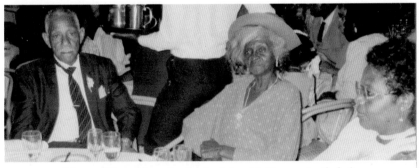

My grandfather and grandmother (seated next to him, wearing the hat)

Aunt Edna and me

Bingo and me

In the living room with my brother Chris

My grandfather and me

My brother Chris and me

My brother Chris with Mom and Dad

My mom and my cousins

My father and me

On the set of my "Twist It" video on Gunit

With Fif at the Vibe awards

My first day at Fif's house in Connecticut, meeting Fifty and Banks and recording

With Dr. Dre at his studio

With my stylist, Misa Hylton, on set after we wrapped the "Candy Shop" video

With Lloyd Banks in Cabo after a performance

Misa Hylton and I overseas in the club

With Shaggy after shooting his video for "Wild 2nite"

On the set of the "Best Friend" video

Me and Fif at MTV

With my LA hairstylist on the set of my photo shoot—Fif watching, LOL!

With John Legend and Alicia Keys

With director Jessy Terrero on set for "Candy Shop"

On the set of the "Twist It" video

My fav cousin Jackie and me

The first time Tarence and I met at the all-white party I hosted

Tarence and I out to dinner in Turkey

Tarence and I celebrating our first New Year together in Turkey, 2011

Out to eat with Chris and Dad

Libbe and I on a reggae cruise back in the day

In the trailer after my Reebok® shoot

My friend Pam Donegan holding my puppy Scooby

Scooby and Shaggy in the back of my car (Yeah, they have on diapers!)

Pam Donegan and me

Pam and her daughter Kylie

Gabrielle and I in Africa, 2008

On the set of *Love & Hip Hop*
season 3 reunion

With my cousin Paul, who used to manage me

Gabrielle and I on the set of a magazine shoot

Me and Tyrese (when we were both signed to J records)

Brandy and me

Me

My dad and Libbe at Jackie's banquet event

Libbe, Jackie, her daughter Tonisha, and I at her banquet event

Jade and me

Me and Fif on the set of "Candy Shop"

With Wyclef at Clive's Grammy party when I first signed to J

Records to deter me and stifle my dream. What if I had gone off the edge and snapped off on some folks like I really wanted to do on the inside? I would have ruined my name and my career. I really would have been out the door on my behind. I might have missed my blessing, because going over to Interscope was how I would be introduced to the hottest rapper on the charts at the time, 50 Cent of G-Unit.

Paul and I were in Los Angeles at the L'Ermitage hotel in Beverly Hills. He hadn't been totally, completely, officially terminated as my manager or anything as of yet. He managed to hang in there at least the first two years of my time with Interscope.

We were just chatting it up in my hotel room when my cell phone rang. I looked down at my caller ID and then answered. "Hey, Chris!" The minute Paul heard me say Chris's name, he came tiptoeing over my shoulder to hear what was going on.

"Wassup, Liv? How's L.A. treating you?" I could hear Chris's big grin through the phone.

"Everything is great. You know I'm loving this weather."

"Oh, I'm sure you are. So, do you have a minute to talk?" he asked.

"Of course I do. It's just me and Paul in here, so talk away."

"Wassup, wassup, C Boogie?" Paul yelled out from the background.

"Cool. 'Sup, brother? Well, as you guys know, I manage 50 Cent." It just so happened that Violator Management also represented 50 Cent. Everything just seemed to be lining up like dominos.

I replied back with, "Okayyy," like, *Where are we going with this?*

"Well, 50 and Dre and I think—"

Before he could even finish the sentence I interrupted. "Wait, you and 50 Cent and Dr. Dre were all talking about me? Together?" The shock was prevalent in my tone.

Chris laughed, "Yes, Olivia. So, can you let me finish?"

I looked at Paul mouthing, "Oh my God!" and then put the call on speaker phone.

Chris proceeded to tell me how they wanted me to join G-Unit. They thought it would be a great branding move.

"So think about the offer seriously, Liv," Chris said, "and get back to me as soon as possible."

How big was that? Here I was in 2003 now signed to Interscope records, then I am approached to do a split deal with 50 Cent. The G-Unit imprint was already signed to Interscope as a subsidiary. Chris made sure I knew this was a monster opportunity and that I would be crazy to pass it up.

Yes, there were many people who would have died for this opportunity and said yes without even thinking twice. As great as everything sounded, this was still a lot to think about. I was a solo R&B artist. Where would I fit in with G-Unit? Would this change my whole image if I signed to G-Unit, and how would this possibly work with me and all these rappers?

The Black Eyed Peas were rising fast at this time, and I tried to compare my situation to theirs, being that Fergie was the only girl in the group and she sang and rapped just like I did. I had a pros and cons list for sure, and I needed to address them all. I decided to speak with 50 Cent myself and tell him I needed a little time to think this over. Chris ended up getting 50 Cent on the line so that we could have a three-way conference call.

"Liv, I got Fif on the line for you," Chris said.

"What's up, girl?" 50 Cent chimed in. "First I wanna say congrats on signing to Interscope."

"Oh my gosh, thank you," I said, trying not to sound as giddy as I was feeling. "I still can't believe I am talking to you right now."

Next came 50 Cent's infamous laugh. "HA HA HA! Aw, man. It's really me, baby."

"Yeah, I can definitely tell that it's really you. You know I am a Queens girl! We gotta put on for our borough."

I know he heard the New York accent coming out, because he then said, "South side all day. Jamaica, Queens raised me. So here's the deal. . . ." He jumped right into it, giving me his ideas about the role I would be playing with G-Unit. He spoke on how Ja Rule and Murder Inc. were on the rise, that we could be bigger than that if I gave it a shot. He boasted about having a foolproof formula. He wanted to take G-Unit far beyond just gangster rap and become a household name. He figured by adding a particular female to the group, it would soften up the image and appeal. See, 50 Cent was known for coming after any and everybody on or off record. He wasn't afraid of anything. He lived for a challenge. 50 Cent can be very convincing, I will tell you that.

"Man, it all sounds good," I said after he gave me his plan. "I just need to think this over and talk to my folks. Is it cool if I get back to you? I think this is a serious decision I am about to make, and I don't want to rush and give you an answer without thinking everything through."

He was nothing but nice and agreed to give me all the time I needed. Well, it only took about two weeks. Like I said, I weighed the pros and the cons. At the top of my cons list was safety and being in a group. Then add being in a group with rappers! I may have been a bit skeptical, but I ended up doing the deal. I signed on the dotted line and was a part of a movement that would reign for the next four years.

Chapter 7

Let me hit rewind and go back a couple of years and start off by saying, "Hi, my name is Olivia and I was a player!"

As a pre-teen, my older brother was someone I looked up to, but please don't tell him I said that. I would never hear the end of it. It's safe to say a lot of my hobbies and loves, including working out and sports and the love of every genre of music, is because of him. He has been doing Karate and jiu jitsu since we were kids. He is definitely one of those guys you walk up to in the club and think because he's a pretty boy that he can't fight. Shiiiiit, my brother and his Wesley Snipes "Blade" moves, Chris will put you in a death grip so fast or touch one of your pressure points and have your whole body shut down. My brother is crazy. He takes his Karate craft very seriously. Chris would be up at five in the morning going to the gym when my girlfriends and I were just coming in from the clubs.

My brother was absolutely a popular kid also and straight pretty boy like I mentioned. I mean, that dude got all of the girls, period! He would be dressed so fresh with his flyboy crew. Polo and Tommy Hilfiger was what was popping, and my brother always had those. They all had curly hair or flat tops with designs in their hair. You couldn't tell my brother he wasn't a mack. Funny thing is, he truly was. Man, he had these two friends that looked like Dalvin and Devante from Jodeci. Made me used to wish I was six years older.

Anyway, I guess it was only natural that his little sis would want to be just like him. I started dating at fifteen years old. For the most part, I was always committed to whatever guy I was seeing; that was, until that big brother gene kicked in one day.

I would get home from a movie with one date, have just enough time to change my clothes, and then the next date would be pulling up to take me to dinner. Yeah, I said pulling up. He had to have a car. My dad spoiled me, remember, so if my date couldn't pick me up and bring me back home, it was a no go, boo-boo. This was not the time I wanted my dad to be chauffeuring me.

My player mentality got worse over the years, until I fell in love for the first time ever, or at least what I thought was love. Heck, I was only twenty years old. Not to say that there haven't been many twenty-year-olds, or even younger, who fall in love, marry, and live happily ever after, with wonderful stories to share with their great grandchildren, but that wasn't my story. No, D.A.'s and my story played out a little differently.

I was booked for D.A.'s birthday weekend in Kentucky. All I knew about D.A. was that he was a professional basketball player. That Saturday, I had to show up for a celebrity baseball game D.A. was participating in, and then Saturday night I was to perform at his birthday party. I was told that my being there was supposed to be a surprise for him because he was a big fan of mine. My hit record "Bizounce" had been hot in the streets, so I was told it was a must that I perform that one. I would have been excited to just be singing "Happy Birthday" if I had to. As long as I was doing my thing, with a microphone in my hand, I was in my element.

I was traveling with my security, who was my Uncle Vern and Duane, who is like a big brother. Duane did my hype man stuff with me on stage when I didn't travel with my dancers. Our flight was delayed, so we got into Kentucky late, which made me late getting to the celebrity baseball game, because I had to stop and do a sound check for my performance later. By the time we had changed and gotten to the game it was already halfway over. I got on the field just in time to sign autographs and take a few pictures. My hands didn't even touch the baseball bat, nor did I get a chance to meet the birthday boy. I kept asking Duane if he saw D.A. so that he could at least introduce us before I left to change yet again to be ready for my performance. No such luck. We went back to our hotel rooms and started to get prepared for the festivities.

"Showtime," I said as I hopped into the awaiting limo, ready to take us over to the venue.

"O to the L-I, V to the I . . . Hip-hop hooraaaayyyy," Duane chanted in the limo, getting his hype man skills started. He was suited up in his one-piece spray-painted jumper. "You ready, li'l sis? It's a bunch of B-ballers out here waiting to get down tonight." Duane was so hype, all the more reason why he was my hype man. He loved his job.

Uncle Vern just shook his head at the two of us. "All right, we can go now, driver."

I hadn't forgotten about Duane and his inquiry. "You know I stay ready, so I ain't got to get ready, bruh." I always had to have a catch phrase going on.

Duane and I talked mess until we pulled into the parking lot of the venue.

"I will be right back, Miss Livy. I'm going to check out our dressing room section and then I will be back out to get you guys," Uncle Vern said. Uncle Vern had already done head security detail for B2K and Faith Evans, so he was very professional. Plus, he was my godfather. He always treated me like a daughter.

After making sure everything was decent and in order, Uncle Vern came back to get us and walked us to the dressing room. "Okay, look, there is no stage where they have you guys performing, because they wanted you to only perform on the VIP side. The main dance floor is where the stage was at, but we are in a private hall area, where you can see the main section across the way."

This wasn't like back in the day when I wanted people to turn away if I sang. I was in the big league now, in my element. I wanted to shine, and I wanted everyone within my radius to see the shine. Duane and I decided that we were going to make our own stage, so everyone could get a chance to see me perform.

Now, picture my little ass performing and standing on chairs and tables. I don't even remember how I ended up getting on those chairs. I think everyone was so damn tall, considering the celebration was for a baller. I wanted to be at eye level.

"I'm about to bizounce. I can't take this shit no more," I sang. "Picture frame broken, daddy, 'cause I can't trust you. I'm riding high now . . ."

I held the mic toward the crowd and then they finished with, "So, nigga, f—you."

Once I got finished, the back of my top was soaked with sweat. "I was kicking it like it was my damn birthday," I said to Duane as I wiped the sweat off of me with a towel Uncle Vern had waiting for me. "Man, I'm having a good time. You would think I was the one celebrating," I said into the mic. "Speaking of which, where is the birthday boy?"

"Here I go."

I looked up, and there was D.A. cheesing all hard, with his hands in his suit pants. He had on an all-white suit with a black shirt underneath and black dress shoes. I noticed him staring at me during the performance and knew who he was by then, because I had seen all the flyers before we got there with his face on them.

"Let me help you down," he said, reaching out his hand.

"Why, thank you, Prince Charming," I said as he helped me down off the chairs.

By this time, Uncle Vern had seen the eye contact between us, so he formally introduced us.

"Miss Livy," Uncle Vern said with his Southern charm, which was only natural considering he was from the South, "I would like to introduce you to Derek Anderson."

"Nice to meet you, Mr. Anderson." I blushed.

"The pleasure is all mine." He smiled before a couple of his boys came over and started talking to him.

I don't remember speaking that much to him for the rest of the night, but I did notice D.A. and Uncle Vern chatting it up. It was about fifteen minutes after my performance when we decided to hit the road. Duane and I got back in the limo as Uncle Vern walked out talking to D.A.'s boys.

"Man, that was fun as hell," Duane said, wiping the sweat from his brow because he had been dancing on the table next to me.

"Yo, we are crazy. We know how to turn up a party. They weren't expecting us to do all that, but hey, if it would have been a real stage in the VIP section, I don't think we would have been that creative."

"For sure," Duane agreed, and then Uncle Vern finally made his way to the limo.

"Livy, do you know who this guy is?" Uncle Vern said, getting into the limo all excited.

Apparently Uncle Vern did know him, because he proceeded to run down to me D.A.'s entire biography. "He went to the University of Kentucky, where he helped his team win an NCAA championship. At first he played for the Cleveland Cavaliers and the L.A. Clippers. Eventually he started playing for the Blazers. Man, this guy is good. He has a great reputation on and off the court."

Even being the huge sports fan that I was, I wasn't too knowledgeable about Derek Anderson, because he wasn't on one of the teams I faithfully followed. He was currently playing for the Portland Trailblazers.

"Well, would you like to tell me what his favorite foods are and if he likes to take long walks on the beach, Uncle Vern?" I said sarcastically, smirking.

"My point is he asked if you would come by his house tomorrow for lunch so he could talk with you," Uncle Vern said. "Trust me, Ms. Livy, he is one of the good guys."

I loved me some Uncle Vern and trusted him with my life, but I was very hesitant and wanted to know why Uncle Vern was trying to play matchmaker. He normally kept the guys away from me, but here he was trying to give me away. "Okay, Uncle Vern, what's really going on? Why you acting like you're his cheerleader or something? What point are you trying to make? Did you make a bet with somebody? This is so unlike you." I gave him the side eye.

"Listen, he is digging you. A blind man could see that. And I think I saw you blushing a couple times."

"Man, I had on blush, Uncle Vern. You tripping." I put my head down and began blushing again. "So, that doesn't mean anything."

"Mm-hmm. See there," Uncle Vern said, pointing at me.

"Okay, okay, so he's a'ight," I said, playing it down. I had to admit that there was a little vibe going on between us for that little bit of time we had been in each other's presence.

"So go out with him," Uncle Vern reasoned, his tone damn near insisting. "We will only be there a little while, and you aren't going alone, I told him I would be with you," he continued. "All you have to do is say yes."

I paused and looked over at Duane. He just shrugged and had this look on his face that said, "My name is Bennett, and I ain't in it."

"Well?" Uncle Vern said with his impatient self.

I rolled my eyes up in my head and finally gave in. "Yes, I'll go out with this D.A." Lord, what was this world coming to, me letting my uncle hook me up?

Uncle Vern set it up for us to hang out the next day before we headed back to New York. Uncle Vern sure enough was with me. I was not about to go out by myself with a stranger. NBA star or not, Papa ain't raise no fool. I needed to be under supervision. But it was all good. Derek didn't take it the wrong way. He told Uncle Vern he wanted me to be comfortable. He showed up at the hotel with his boy to pick us up.

The hotel receptionist called up to my room to let me know that my guest was waiting out in front of the hotel for me. I hit Uncle Vern up, and we headed downstairs and out of the hotel lobby. You couldn't miss Derek. He was in the only shiny white four-door Bentley out front. His friend Greg, whom I'd briefly met at the party the night before, was behind him in one of Derek's other cars.

Once Derek saw me, he got out of the driver's seat and walked around to the passenger side. "Good to see you again, Miss Olivia," he said, opening the door for me.

"Likewise," I said, playing up that same Southern charm he had. He looked to Uncle Vern. "My boy Greg is right there behind us." He pointed to the white Escalade. "You can roll with him. I promise I'll take good care of her." He winked at me.

Uncle Vern looked at me, awaiting my approval. I nodded and then he made his way back to the car with Greg. Derek closed the door and then got back into the driver's seat.

"You ready?" he asked me, putting the car in drive.

"Born ready," I shot then looked straight ahead as we headed to our destination. "Where are we going anyway?" I asked as we drove.

"I just figured I could show you around Kentucky then hang out at my place, if that's okay with you."

"Mm-hmm. I see how you NBA stars do it," I teased. "That's why I got Uncle Vern with me," I said, laughing.

He joined in on the laughter. "No, ma'am, it ain't even like that. I have my son and friends at the house, and I had my chef prepare lunch. You can trust me."

"Hmm, well, obviously you're the one who is scared." I nodded to the car following us. "You done brought your boy along to protect you." His boy Greg was about as tall as he was, six feet five inches, and a bit wider than uncle Vern was. Uncle Vern weighed about 300 pounds back then, so add a few pounds to that—like forty! Greg was all Derek needed when he walked out the door. "What did you think little ol' me was going to do to you?"

"Little ol' you nothing," he said. "I saw you going in last night at the party. You dangerous." He smiled.

I smiled back. After that we just pretty much had small talk up until we got closer to his crib.

As we turned onto his block, the homes looked like pictures straight out of an *Architectural Digest* magazine—huge columns, gorgeous brick work, well-manicured lawns. My eyes were so wide from the view. We finally headed up a private driveway that I assumed was his place. There was lots of land.

"Are those your horses too?" I pointed upon noticing some horses encaged by a fence. They had these huge stables. It was just gorgeous. "Wow, they look like statues of stallions."

He gave me the politest, "Yes, ma'am," response I had ever heard, while flashing that charming smile. He is probably one of the reasons why I like country accents to this day.

Upon parking and getting out of the car, we stood outside for a minute and waited for Greg and Uncle Vern to join us.

"So all of that over there is my land." He pointed to the area where the horses were and beyond.

"Wow, this is really amazing, man," Uncle Vern said as he walked up next to me.

"Thank you," Derek said. "Come on. Let's go inside."

We walked in through the side door, which led to the kitchen. I studied the beautiful marble counters and floors. Even the kitchen table was elegant. Everything looked so regal and clean, and just like he said, there was a spread of food on the counters that his chef had prepared.

"Come on. Let me show you around," Derek said.

"I'll stay here with Greg," Uncle Vern replied. "You guys go ahead." Uncle Vern waved me off and gave me a wink. I think Uncle Vern just wanted to get to that food! All I could do was shake my head at Mr. Matchmaker himself as Derek took me on a tour of his casa.

"Well, here's the living room," he said.

I gave the room a once over and looked up, noticing a huge staircase that took up half of the center of the second floor.

"I love staircases. I always wanted a huge spiral staircase in my home," I said.

Derek led me upstairs, where there were three huge bedrooms. "This one is the master," he said, escorting me inside the room.

"Damn, this is bigger than most people's entire crib. And the décor is bananas. You really have some good taste."

He looked me up and down. "I sure do." He winked at me.

"You are something else. Very funny," I said, trying not to blush, but the chemistry between the two of us was undeniable.

A few minutes later we were on the last leg of the tour.

"And last but not least, this is the basement." He spread his arms out for me to take in the incredible space.

"You have got to be kidding me," I said, turning around to take everything in. "If I lived here, I would never leave the house, let alone this room." The basement was incredible. It had both a mini bowling alley and a home theater.

He laughed at me as I began to spin around like Alice in Wonderland. "Yeah, it's kinda hard for me some days too."

We stayed in the basement so we could talk uninterrupted.

"So, do you have a man?" Derek asked, cutting right to the chase for real.

"Good first question," I replied. "I wouldn't be here if I did," I said with a smirk.

"Well, that's good news."

We stared at each other for a minute. I got out of his trance just in time to ask him a question. "Um, I see you are a big fan of loyalty?" I was referring to the flyers for his birthday party that had *Loyalty* written on the back of them, and a Trailblazers jersey with *Loyalty* and *#1* that was hanging on his wall.

"Oh, yeah. That's what my whole organization is about." He got very serious. "I can't have people around me I can't trust and who aren't loyal."

Noticing how serious he was about the topic, I said, "I hear that. It seems to me you are a straightforward, clean-cut guy."

"Oh, yes, ma'am. God has been too good to me, so I take care of the people who have always been loyal. I read

the Bible every day. I carry it everywhere with me." My
face lit up because I, too, took my Bible everywhere. I
packed it in my suitcase every road trip.

I was starting to like him more and more with every
word that came out of his mouth. A man after God's
own heart and not after every piece of tail he could get
definitely was not the average description you hear when
people discuss an NBA player. In my eyes, right there at
that moment, Derek was the exception. He was so sweet
and the most charming man I had ever met in my twenty
years. It was at that very moment that I became smitten.

"I hate to break up the party." I immediately recognized
Uncle Vern's voice. I looked up to see him coming down
the steps. "But, Livy, we have to get to the airport."

I let out a big sigh. "You sure we have to leave, Uncle
Vern?" It was obvious I was not ready to leave Kentucky
or the man responsible for my being there . . . and not in
that order.

"As much as I don't want to go either," he looked
around, "'cause being in this place is like being in heaven,
yeah, Miss Livy, you've got an appearance in New York
tomorrow."

I tried to hide the disappointment on my face. "All
right. Give me a minute to say good-bye, then we'll be
right up."

"All right," Uncle Vern said as he went back up the
steps.

"Well, I guess I have to go." I put my head down and
poked out my lips, doing an overexaggerated pout.

"Dang, I know how you feel. I wish you didn't have
to go either. I've really enjoyed your company. I feel so
natural around you."

"Same here. I know it's crazy, right," I agreed. "Not to
sound all cliché and like a cornball, but where have you
been my entire life?" We both burst out laughing.

We headed upstairs. Uncle Vern, Greg, and a couple of his other boys were all huddled up at the kitchen table looking like they had just gotten finished talking about us. You know, it was one of those instances where we could hear all kinds of chattering and laughing from a distance, but the minute we walked into the room it all stopped. Neither Derek nor I called them on it, though. Derek just proceeded to introduce me to his friends.

After the meet and greet, it was about time to head out. We still had to go back to the hotel and get our stuff.

"It was such a pleasure meeting you guys," I said to everyone.

"You trying to get rid of us already, Miss Lady?" Greg said.

I laughed. "Of course not. I'm actually trying to convince Uncle Vern to stay." I nudged Uncle Vern on the arm with my elbow while winking and saying, "Hint, hint."

"Like I said," Uncle Vern reiterated, "I wish we could, but you know you have an appearance tomorrow."

"I know, I know," I said. "Guess we really do need to head out." I looked at Derek. "You ready to take us back to the hotel?"

"You do know I am taking you to the airport as well, right?" Derek said with his charming smile. "I'm trying to get in every moment I can with you."

Mr. Derek Anderson was just too much for this Queens girl. I was blushing so hard I thought the force of my batting eyes were going to be like wings and I'd take off flying any minute.

We walked out to the cars, and Derek opened the door for me with his Southern hospitality. Y'all know the saying: Ladies, if a man can't even open the door for you, how are you going to open your legs for him?

"Hey, guys," Uncle Vern said. "Greg said he'd drive me. That way y'all can get some more alone time in."

I wanted to run over and give Uncle Vern the biggest hug in the world for that one.

We all got into our vehicles and headed back to the hotel. I took one last glance at the house and his beautiful horses on the way out, thinking, *I could get used to this.*

Chapter 8

I can't even describe the melancholy feeling I had in the pit of my stomach as Derek drove us away from his house. I just stared out of the window all sad, like some kid being taken away from their home by children's services.

As we passed by the horses on the way out, I said, "Your horses are just gorgeous. I've never seen anything like this before. I wish I could have ridden them."

"Well, we will have to fix that the next time you come back."

Now, that comment perked a doll up. We looked over at each other and smiled.

"Do you want to listen to a little music?"

"Sure." I nodded.

He put in a CD and turned up the music. I knew distinctively who it was.

"What do you know about Dave Hollister, boy? I love him." I started snapping my fingers and rocking a little bit.

The next thing I knew, I heard someone joining in on Dave's vocals. "Where would I go, what would I do, do without you? I'm not complete unless you're with me." He shot me a smug look. "Dave Hollister, baby. *Chicago 85* album." He reached his hand out.

I looked down at his awaiting hand and, of course, I put my hand in his. I stared at our hands clasped together tightly, like we were already a budding couple.

After a few minutes, still holding hands, we were both singing, "We've come too far to give up on us." It was like a scene from *Titanic*. As corny as it may all seem, it was the beginning of something special. I could see that already.

We got back to the hotel and Uncle Vern, Duane and I checked out of the hotel. On the ride to the airport, both Duane and Uncle Vern rode with Greg, while I rode with Derek.

"Best ride to the airport ever," I whispered as we pulled up at the airport. "I really don't want to get out of this car."

"I don't want to see you go either," Derek said with sad, puppy-dog eyes. "But I'm absolutely going to watch when you walk away."

I just shook my head and laughed. "You are too cute."

"But for real, when can I see you again?" he asked.

"I have to check my schedule. I'm usually performing every weekend and traveling during the week, but trust me when I say that you will be the first to know."

Both Duane and Uncle Vern were already out of the car with their luggage, waiting on the curb for me to get out of the car. With Uncle Vern surely looking at us out of the corner of his eye, Derek went in for the kiss anyway. It was a nice, soft peck. Just enough to taste each other's lips. As small as it was, it was just enough to keep me blushing.

No matter how badly I wanted to, I was not about to tongue kiss this man in front of Uncle Vern. He was like a father figure. Way too awkward. So for now, a chaste peck would have to suffice.

Once I returned to New York, Derek and I talked every day and very quickly became a couple. At times it was frustrating because I wanted to be with him more often, but because of my schedule I couldn't. He made sure to tell me that he hated me not being at certain games and even made fun, saying, "Why can't you just stop singing so you can be at all my games?"

Even though he called himself joking, I could tell there was some seriousness behind it by the way he would try to read me after making the comment. Well, you know I didn't like that comment. Besides, if it hadn't been for my job, I would have never even met him in the first place.

When I left J Records and signed with G-Unit, Derek hated that even more. He didn't like the fact that I now had to be around all this violence, not to mention all those dudes. We were riding around Kentucky in his car, and he started the conversation about my safety.

"I really am uncomfortable with you being around guns," he said. It was no secret that on tour, some people were strapped—all for protection purposes, of course.

"But, babe, you carry one in your toiletry bag when you're going to the games," I said sarcastically.

"That is very different and you know it. I've seen guys get stuck up or tested after the games. I am protecting me and mines. I don't bring violence around us. I am just prepared if the situation arises. Plus, I'm licensed, dear," he said back in the same sarcastic tone.

"Okay, look," I said, trying to calm things down so they didn't get out of hand. "I can tell you are really concerned, but when I tour with the guys, we drive around in bullet-proof trucks. Nothing is going to happen to me. I know it sounds scary, but to be honest, I'm used to it now."

"Well, I don't want my woman around all the stuff. It's too dangerous. I don't know what I would do if—"

I cut him off before he could finish. "Don't even think like that, baby. Everything is going to be fine. I will see what I can do to make you more comfortable when I'm on the road."

But like I said, even getting past the issues with me being the only female around all those other guys didn't do anything to ease Derek's concerns about my safety.

Derek had good cause, though, to worry about my safety. Hell, I worried about it sometimes, especially one time in particular, when we had just performed in Lagos, Nigeria at a huge outdoor venue. I promise you, and it's no exaggeration, that I saw my life flash before my eyes.

G-Unit had murdered the performance, as usual, and was heading back to the States. 50 and I were a bit skeptical when a few people started throwing their shoes on stage, but afterward the locals told us that it was a sign of respect, their way of showing they loved us. That is a different sign of respect than I ever would have guessed. Those flying shoes caught us off guard a few times. At one point, 50 threw a shoe back in the crowd. We were cracking up. Man, we had no idea what it meant. We just knew a lot of people were going home barefoot that night.

Heading over to the airport, we were being driven to the runway in two separate SUVs. The one 50 and I were in was bulletproof, because that's just how 50 rolled: bulletproof vest and bulletproof vehicle. Buck and Banks were in the SUV behind us, but it wasn't bulletproof. Yayo was back in the States because his criminal record prevented him from leaving the country. There was security in both vehicles and extra security in the truck that was leading us to airport.

By the time our vehicles arrived at the plane, all of the other passengers had already boarded from inside the terminal. No worries, though, because we had bought out the entire first class, so our empty seats were waiting for us. We knew we wouldn't have to bump into people and try to find overhead space for our carry-ons and whatnot. Our bags were always transported ahead of us in a separate vehicle.

Two of the security guards boarded the plane before us. When 50 and I stepped on the plane, there was a gentleman seated in first class. A member of the airline crew was talking to him, while the two members of our security staff stood beside her.

"Like I said, sir," the airline crew member said to the gentleman sitting in the seat, "these seats are reserved. You are going to have to go sit in your assigned seat."

"I ain't moving nowhere," he spat with his Nigerian accent.

"Then you are about to get moved," one of our security guards said. "This is like the VIP section in a club, and you belong back there in general admission." He pointed back toward coach.

"Man, fuck that," the Nigerian shouted.

It was clear that things were about to get ugly. One of our security guards walked over to 50 and me. Without saying a word, he edged us back toward the cockpit. I guess he figured things were about to go wrong as well. Buck and Banks hadn't even gotten on the plane yet. After security made sure 50 and I were secure, he walked back over to the commotion.

"That fool ain't shit." The man continued his rant. "Why I gotta move for G-Unit? I ain't have to move for Busta or Wyclef. Fuck that. I ain't moving nowhere." He looked at our security as if he could spit on them any minute. "And fuck y'all too."

This clown was going off. Now, I could see if he had paid for a first class seat; then obviously he would have had grounds to be running his mouth. But like I said, G-Unit had bought out the entire section. He was acting like we'd charged it to his Black Card or something. He just kept going on and on. Our security was more than patient with this guy at first, but eventually playtime was over.

He done did it now! The next thing I knew, arms were swinging. Our security kind of pushed the airline crew member out of the way and went in on ol' dude. One yoked him up out of his seat, and they both proceeded to escort him off the plane. You would have thought it was a scene out of the video game Mortal Kombat the way they had buddy hemmed up with uppercuts and choke holds. After they got the troublemaker off the plane, our other security escorted 50 and I back off the plane.

Airport security arrived on the scene and asked us to go back and wait in our vehicles until everything was under control. They were sending another plane for us. We all headed back to our respective SUVs, shaking our heads like, "This is some bullshit!" Dude was out of control.

"This just the fuck why I hate flying commercial," 50 said as we got back in our vehicle. "I knew I should have gone with my first instincts and arranged for the private jet."

We had a total of six security guards on payroll. There was one inside each car and two outside of each vehicle. Eventually more airport security showed up, as well as government-assigned security.

50 was regretting taking a commercial flight. After a while, he was back laughing and put his headphones on with music blasting from them. We were both looking out the truck windows aimlessly, waiting for someone to come tell us how much longer we would have to wait here. It had already been more than forty-five minutes by now.

"Oh, shit," the security guard inside our vehicle said under his breath.

I started looking around to see what brought on his comment. I tapped 50 to take his headphones off. The security guard was looking behind the truck at the other guards to see if they were seeing this shit. Now, of course, 50 and I were both looking up at what seemed to be a

Nigerian gang takeover! We saw this Jeep rolling up full of Nigerians. A gang of them were walking toward our vehicles, with the dude that had been in our seat on the plane as the ringleader. Another slew of people rolled up behind them.

There was a huge cement wall that separated the runway and waiting aircraft from the main terminal of the airport. Well, the Nigerian guy actually had some of his boys climbing over that freakin' wall. Between the guys in the Jeep and the ones climbing over the walls, they were carrying guns and bats. Shit was insane. No way was this real.

I kept asking myself where all that post 9-11 security was when we needed it. Then I remembered that I was not in the United States. This was Nigeria, and I had no idea how they did things. Obviously they didn't do too much of nothing for these dudes to be able to roll up on us like that.

I could hear my heart beating so loud I just knew my eardrums were about to erupt any minute. Security was straight-faced, with their own weapons drawn and cocked. 50 was even cool.

In my head, I was like, *Chill. They got this.* The next minute I would be like, *Am I the only one seeing this? Is this real? Did I actually board the plane, fall asleep, and all of this is a nightmare?*

I looked at 50 like, "Dude, it's about to go down and you chilling?"

He read the expression on my face and simply touched my hand, laughed, and said, "What? We cool. We in a bulletproof Jeep." He then looked over his shoulders. "But them mu'fuckas back there." He nodded toward Buck and them's Jeep and as if on cue, shit got real!

Unlike inside our vehicle, where everybody was cool, calm, and collected, Buck and Bank's entourage was back there freaking out. Knowing they didn't have anything protecting them but aluminum and whatever shots those security guards could get off, they were in straight panic mode. I saw one of them climbing into the trunk.

Our security was ready to blaze if need be. They had guns, too, and crow bars. Shit, one of them found a brick. They weren't going down without a fight. The Nigerians were armed and looked damn sure ready to go to war as well. Airport security had their guns drawn. This was like some *Blood Diamond* stuff. I wanted to start shouting, "Our jewelry is legit. No conflict diamonds here!"

50 could see that I was about to lose it. All I could think about was my family and never seeing them again.

"Don't worry, Liv," 50 said. "Ain't nothing about to go down. Trust me. If them fools came to pop off, they would have done it by now. Real gangstas roll up shooting. They ain't about nothing."

For the next few minutes, everyone stood out there reasoning with the Nigerian clan. Finally they were escorted inside. Right after that, the airline representative came over to our vehicle.

"It's going to be about another half hour before we can get you all on another flight, so we're going to ask that you all come inside."

Our security and airport security escorted us back inside the airport. We all sat in the airport tripping over the situation. We saw the Nigerian ringleader being escorted in by armed airport security.

"Hey, yo," the Nigerian said to 50 as if he knew him personally, as if all that drama hadn't just gone down twenty minutes ago. "Yo, let me get a picture. Come on, man. Let me get a picture with G-Unit."

Okay, now we were all really looking crazy, giving each other the look like, "Is this dude for real?"

"Is that dude for real?" 50 ended up actually saying to a police officer that walked up on the scene.

"Unfortunately, he's dead serious," the officer replied. I can't remember what it was, but he called the man by name. "We're quite familiar with that goon," the officer said to us, referring to the ringleader. "He's some wannabe rapper. He's always pulling some kind of crazy stunt to try to make a name for himself." He then looked at my nervous self. "In spite of what it looks like, trust me, he's harmless. All he wants is to end up in the papers and on the news so that people will know his name."

Of course 50 gave me the I-told-you-so-look. "And that is the definition of a wanksta."

All I could do was shake my head.

Believe it or not, ol' dude got just what he wanted. He made the news and was all in the papers. He looked like a fool in the write up and they didn't have anything positive to say about ol' buddy. Crazy people think any publicity is good publicity. I beg to differ.

I had to admit, when I signed on the dotted line with G-Unit, I had no idea just exactly what I was signing up for. Show after show, city after city, there was always some kind of drama to write home about. With all the beef in the industry and me being connected to G-Unit, Derek's fears were legitimate. He had reason to be concerned, and obviously so did Chris Lighty.

One day Chris had come to visit us backstage before one of our shows. "Liv," he said with this mischievous smile he threw on us every once in a while. We knew that whenever he hit us with that smile something slick or fishy was about to follow. "I got something for you." He held up a bag teasingly.

All excited, thinking it's a purse or a pair of shoes since he knew how much I loved those things, I was like, "What is it? Can I wear it on my set?"

"Funny you should say that. I want you to wear it on the set." He laughed as he pulled out a pink bulletproof vest for me. "POW!"

"What the . . . You can't be serious, Christopher," I said with my arms folded.

"What?" He gave me this look like I was the one talking crazy. "This is a great idea. 50 wears a vest as part of his set during 'I'm Supposed to Die Tonight' and 'In My Hood.'"

"Ughhh." I held up the vest and just looked at it with disgust. Now, to one of the guys this would have been a perfectly normal idea, but I'm flashing back to Derek being worried about my safety. In my head I'm thinking, *Does Chris think someone is going to try to shoot us during our set?* My mind completely went left field, and I was one hundred percent with Derek's concerns now.

I handed the vest back to Chris. "I'm good, Chris. I don't need to wear that, but thank you . . . I guess." I shook my head and poured myself a cup of hot tea to calm my nerves. I heard the door close behind me, and when I turned around, Chris was gone, but the vest still lay there staring at me. That vest was going to sit right there, because Olivia did not put it on. He tried it, but I was not going for it.

I honestly can't say if the whole wearing a bulletproof vest idea made Derek feel more comfortable or worse, but what I did know was that I didn't want him feeling a certain kind of way. I really cared for him and wanted to please and make him happy. He was the first man to keep me faithful. I never once thought about being a player with him. How ironic that he was an NBA star, considering the stigma attached to them being players (and not just ball players).

Derek and I managed to maintain a decent relationship for a few years. At first everything seemed so perfect. He was such a gentleman, loved God, and he was tall and handsome. I couldn't have asked for a better relationship. But like the saying goes, all good things must come to an end. Now, I really don't like to use that saying, because I do believe that if it is meant to last, it will.

It wasn't cheating or anything like that that caused our relationship to start to deteriorate. There was no domestic violence or bad habits neither of us couldn't deal with. What ultimately began to push us further apart was distance and our careers.

My singing career meant everything to me. Singing and music had been a part of my life since I was yea high, so I could not bring myself to choose Derek over it. Derek really didn't like that I couldn't just come and see him at the drop of a dime. I would have expected him to understand because of his hectic schedule, but NBA players have an off season. The music business is all year round! It broke my heart that we couldn't come to an agreement and try to work things out, but in the end he just didn't want to deal with it anymore. He had had enough of my always traveling, doing my thing, trying to make it big, so he told me he wanted to break things off.

Initially I didn't know if he was bluffing or what. All I knew is that I loved him and absolutely did not want to call things off. I gave him all the reasons why we shouldn't break up, while he gave me all the reasons why we should. His reasons boiled down to him wanting his woman by his side. He was the man, and he wanted to take care of everything.

Now, if I was a stay at home mom or someone who didn't have a career and was content being a housewife, then he would have been in luck. How can you let my career stand in the way of our love? I just couldn't comprehend that. Not in a million years would I have ever asked him to give up basketball so he could be at all of my concerts. For Derek, though, the time I could give him just wasn't enough.

On top of everything, this breakup took place over the phone. That's like the lamest thing next to a breakup text.

I cried after we got off the phone. As a matter of fact, I drove to Libbe's house and she consoled me—you know, gave me the whole "It's him, not you" speech. We finished a bottle of wine together while we ate our favorite cheese, Parmigiano-Reggiano, and green olives. She knew how to cheer me up with my favorites.

For the next two weeks, I'd find myself in this sad place. Music was the only thing that eased my pain. It was time to get back on the road, and being on stage was what I did best, so this doll had to pull it together and put on a show for the world, all while my heart was hurting. But you know me; Olivia keeps it moving. I picked up the pieces of my disappointed heart from my first long distance relationship. In my mind, I knew that he wouldn't be the last. Convincing my heart of that was the problem.

But don't go weeping for me, because like I stated in the beginning, I was a player, so I went right back to what I did second best—dating and crushing hearts (After I got him out of my system, of course).

The only thing good that came out of that relationship was my second family, the Donegans. I met Pam right at the beginning of our relationship. She was a concierge for the Blazers. The first time I ever went to Portland to see D.A., she met me at the airport.

"Hi, is this Olivia?" said an unfamiliar voice over the phone

"Yes, it is, and who am I speaking to?" I asked as I stood at the baggage claim carousel.

"This is Pam Donegan, and I am a concierge for the Portland Trailblazers. Derek asked me to pick you up because they are still in practice." She sounded so darn friendly over the phone.

"Okay, great. Well, I am just grabbing my bag off the carousel and I will be right out."

"Oh, take your time. I am parked right in front when you walk out. I'm in a white Range Rover."

With luggage in tow, I walked out and saw the cutest little blond-haired, beautiful blue-eyed woman waiting for me.

"Pam?" I had to be sure I wasn't just jumping into any ol' body's truck.

"Yes, my darling." She got out and gave me the sweetest hug.

We got acquainted as we drove to a restaurant to get some food. I was starving from that five-hour flight. By the end of our meal, I didn't want to let Pam go. She was as crazy and fun as I was, and such a sweetheart! I loved her after meeting her for the first time. There would be many trips that I traveled to Portland where I would make sure I spent time with Pam and her family. Her husband Mark was very well off and Pam really didn't have to work a day in her life if she didn't want to. Lucky little devil.

We would be riding around their neighborhood in her golf cart, making honking noises at people because the cart didn't have a horn. I mean, we just had too much fun when we were together. One time we found ourselves going to the gym. We really were going to work out, I swear, but we had gotten on the treadmill and our view was suddenly obstructed.

"Um, three o'clock, Olivia, incoming," Pam had said, dying with laughter.

Naturally I looked over to see what the hell was so funny. "Oh my God, Pam, is that what I think it is?" I was now crying in laughter.

There stood this older muscular man in little Speedos and a tank top. His junk was swoll', staring right at us like it needed to get out of his shorts for some air. It was disgusting and hilarious at the same time. We couldn't even begin to focus on working out. Let's just say he creeped us out so bad that we left and went shopping!

Pam was like that aunt or big sister who always gets you into trouble but you have so much fun with them that you don't care. Anytime Pam and her family came to New York, we would meet up and hang out. To this day she is still family. Her daughter, Kylie, recently had a baby and I gave them his name. I am so glad she asked me for help, because baby Kingston would have hated the name they had in mind for the little guy had I not intervened. You can thank Aunty Livy when you get older, King.

I recall watching Pam and her husband Mark together, loving how fun and carefree she was and how he was always there to reel her back in if she got carried away. Mark knows Pam is crazy and he loves it. He is more on the serious side, but they balance each other out. Mark's business had him in and out of town a lot, but they make their relationship work just fine. Pam works when or if she wants, even though she doesn't have to.

I will never understand why some men would rather have their woman sit at home and do nothing. I used to wonder what the heck I would have done if I quit my career to stay at home and just attend Derek's games . . . in my early twenties! I had no idea that women had to choose between their love lives and their careers. Some men expect to be the breadwinners and assume the woman will just stay home raising kids and cleaning. Well, the last time I checked, women are amazing and can do anything men can do, period—and half the time do it better!

If I wanted to have a career, I was going to do just that without letting anything get in my way . . . even love. Like Tina said, baby, "What's love got to do with it?"

I would think most men could deal with having a woman who worked outside of the home. That means she has her own to some degree, and he wouldn't have to worry about paying all the bills. In a way, though, I could see where Derek was coming from. He was old school and wanted to take care of what was his. I respected that and never got in the way of him being a man. It's just that I wanted his love more than his house, horses, and anything else material. Hell, I could get that on my own.

Derek wanted a family. I did, too, but he had to recognize that I was not built to be June Cleaver. Once I dropped the load, I was going to lose all that baby weight and be back on the road touring. He would not have been able to deal with that.

I'm sorry, but Olivia's life can't stop to pacify the male ego. Life is too short for that. Besides, a real man is secure enough in himself to let a woman do what she needs to do. There is always this rah-rah about how a woman needs to be her man's cheerleader. I get that. But whatever happened to a man supporting his woman?

As always, this was just one more thing in which I had to find my lesson. What I learned was that the next man better not even think about asking me to choose between my career and my relationship with him. If he truly loves and supports me, then I shouldn't have to choose.

Since I was making my "list," I decided to really go for what I wanted in a man.

I want a man who will bring me flowers just because it's Tuesday, no special occasion at all. I want a man who is going to cook for me when I get home from a long day's work. If he can't cook, takeout will do just fine. Set the table, play some soft music, put rose petals on the floor every once in a while. Be interesting. Take me out to the movies. Shoot, we can even stay home and watch a movie. And there is nothing like a man who every now and then wants to sit and watch sports with me instead of his boys.

I don't think that's asking a lot. In short, I just need a man to remind me why I am with him. Tell me how beautiful I am. It doesn't matter how many people tell a woman she is beautiful; it's nothing like hearing it from her own man. And most importantly, I love a man with old school manners. Pull out my chair, open doors for me; tell me I look good in that dress. Manners and a sincere compliment go a long way.

I don't think everything needs to be one-sided. As a woman, I know I have needs to meet as well. I love to spoil my significant other. That's just the type of person I am. I am very affectionate, attentive, and I love surprising my man every once in a while with gifts just because.

One time I caught myself being romantical—yes, I said *romantical*. Y'all read it right. I wanted to do something sweet for a guy I was dating. I put rose petals going up the stairs leading to the bathroom. When he entered the bathroom, there were candles surrounding the Jacuzzi and on the counters. Hey, a man wants to feel special too.

Every woman has heard that one way to a man's heart is definitely through his stomach. So, even though I don't always have the time to throw down in the kitchen, I can cook my butt off. My grandfather was a chef, and he taught my father, who taught me. Still, I do know how to get takeout and can damn sure set the table . . . if you know what I mean.

Chapter 9

I'd landed on the G-Unit record label in late 2003, and by 2005 we were on our first international tour. I think we were in Monaco or somewhere. I felt so spoiled, because it was just me, the only girl, being treated like a princess by everyone.

I really got spoiled with my Reebok Women deal. See, 50 Cent was a marketing genius. He'd already had the men's line doing well, and when I came along, he suggested that it only made sense to do a G-Unit women's line. I got a check for that endorsement deal, was the face of the line, and I got free kicks. I had boxes of every sneaker you can think of, in every color, coming in each month. Then I got to custom make them with the O's on it. What! You couldn't tell me I wasn't Orville Redenbacher himself, popping! I had a different sneaker on the road every day. Killing 'em, you hear me!

I was in my early 20s now, so this was the life for me. Because I was getting so much stuff for free for myself, that left room for me to finally be able to buy my mom that expensive ticket item I'd been waiting to purchase for her all those years.

I walked into this store like I was ready to buy the entire place. I had my cousin Jackie with me. I took Jackie everywhere because she was my assistant.

"Do you need any help?" one of the clerks in the store walked over to us and asked.

"Yes, ma'am," I replied. "I'd love it if you could show me some fabulous furs."

"I'm scared of you, Miss First Lady of G-Unit," Jackie teased. "I guess you gon' be styling for real."

The smile on my face matched the huge one on hers as I thought about what I was going to do with that fur. "No, I'm getting it for Mommy," I proudly stated. I'd been waiting since the days of watching her spin around in the mirrors at Macy's to finally be able to buy my mom something as lavish as this. Well, today was the day.

"How sweet," the clerk said. "Is it her birthday or something?"

"No, it's just because," I said.

In no time at all the clerk and another woman she got to help her brought out a few pieces for me to look at. This one piece in particular caught my eye. "Jackie, Mommy will love this," I exclaimed with my eyes all bright. It was the prettiest shade of peach/coral I had ever seen. Soft and pretty, just like my mommy.

"It's sheepskin," the clerk pointed out.

"Try this on, J," I turned and said to Jackie, handing her the fur. "You and Mommy are about the same size."

Jackie slid into that baby and twirled around in that fur so much that she had us all dizzy!

"Okay, all right already," I said, laughing. "J, it fits. We get it. You love it, but my mommy is going to love it more. Now take it off," I said with a smirk and sarcastic tone.

As Jackie took the fur off, her face was all sad and broken up. I thought she was about to cry. She was acting like she had carried me for nine months and deserved the "just because" gift.

The clerk finally managed to take possession of the fur. "Would you like it wrapped?"

"Yes, ma'am!" I was too excited. Everyone in there really would have thought that fur was for me. But that's just how I was; giving to others and making them happy was the root to my own happiness. I really never needed material things in my life, but I always loved that feeling I got when I gave to others. "Before you wrap it, do y'all happen to have anything else that could accentuate the piece?" As if that fur wasn't enough. "Like a brooch," I added. "My mom loves brooches."

"I'm certain we do. Just one moment." The clerk rushed off to the back of the store. A couple minutes later she returned with the shiniest colored brooch I had ever seen. It was a medium-sized butterfly, and it was glowing all the way from the back before she ever even made it up to the checkout counter.

"It's perfect!" I said once the brooch was resting in my hand. "I'll take that too."

As the clerk rang up everything and told me what the damage would be, I just handed her my credit card with pleasure. I couldn't wait to get back home, knowing that the look on my mom's face would be priceless. Those little smiles I used to try to put on her face when she'd walk through the door after work when I was little wouldn't compare to the smile I knew this baby would produce.

I was so proud that I was able to buy that for her. My mom still only had that one white fur that she used to let me borrow and that she wore to church on occasion. I couldn't wait to add to her collection and see her sporting that bad boy. When we returned home from tour, I couldn't get to my mom and dad's house fast enough. As I walked inside and hugged my parents, I started to tell them about everything we experienced and the many places we traveled to for the first time.

"And y'all know I brought y'all back some souvenirs, right?" I concluded, grabbing the bags I had set at the door while I played catchup with my parents on the couch.

"It better be a fine Cognac in one of those bags for me," my dad said as serious as I don't know what.

I just shook my head. "Of course, Dad. You know I got you." I knew exactly what my pops liked.

As I pulled out the bottle case, my dad rubbed his hands together with a grin that read, "Yeah, baby! Gimme mine!" He was like some big ol' kid.

"Dad, you are crazy." I then turned to my mom. "Come in the bedroom, Ma, 'cause you have to look at yours in the mirror."

She followed me into the bedroom with no idea what I was about to wrap around her pretty little shoulders. I handed her the bag that contained the fur wrapped all nicely in a box.

She sat down and began to unwrap it. She looked up at me with suspicious eyes.

"What?" I asked her.

"I don't know yet, that's what." She rolled her eyes. "Something tells me this is going to be over the top."

"Just open it, Ma." I was so anxious, I was about ten seconds from going over there and opening it up myself.

Once she had all the wrapping off, she opened the box and her mouth fell open. "Oh my goodness, Livy. It's beautiful." She ran her hand down the fur. "But it looks really expensive."

"Don't worry about the price, Ma. Nothing is too expensive for the woman who gave birth to me. Now, pull it out the box and put it on."

She slowly took the fur out of the box as if it were a delicate newborn.

"Allow me to do the honors." My dad walked over and placed the fur around my mother.

From that moment on, I felt like I was that young girl watching my mother try on clothes at Macy's.

"I can't believe you did this, Livy," my mom said.

"You just enjoy it and know that you don't have to worry about nobody else in New York having one of these bad babies. They don't even sell them here. You are going to be stunting."

She pulled it tightly around her. The fur shawl draped down to her knees. The peach color was perfect on her caramel skin.

"Oh, yeah. Wait, Ma. There is one more thing." I reached for the brooch and placed it around the front to close the fur.

She looked down at it. "I love it, baby." Looking up at me with grateful eyes, she said, "You have outdone yourself."

I just smiled and hugged her, knowing she was just as overwhelmed with emotion as I was. I envisioned her prancing around in that fur, getting compliments and responding with, "My baby girl got this for me."

But you know what? To this day I don't think she's ever even worn that fur. At least I've never seen her in it . . . not a picture of her wearing it or anything.

"I'm waiting for a special occasion," she would say whenever I asked her if she was ever going to wear it.

You mean, like to the many fancy dinners you've attended? I thought. *The weddings? Church functions? Or maybe just 'cause it's winter time and that fur can keep three people warm?*

Was she serious? Do you know how many special occasions she could have worn that fur to? I had to smack my forehead like Homer Simpson on that one! *DOH!*

That didn't deter me from still doing nice things for my parents. I wanted to step their restaurant game up from Friendly's and Olive Garden, so I would take them to fine Italian dining, or a really nice, expensive steakhouse. Even with all the different restaurants I exposed them to, one of my dad's favorite restaurants to this day is still the Olive Garden. I can't front, though, because their breadsticks and salads are amazeballs!

When I wasn't treating my family, I loved to treat my friends also. Usually we would split the bill or we would take turns paying for each other, but once I was in the financial position to treat them on the regular, that's exactly what I did.

I was in Whitestone, Queens with Jackie and Libbe. Libbe lived in Whitestone. We were just sitting at the table telling jokes. We'd finished dinner and were munching on cheesecake, our favorite dessert ever.

"And here is your check, ladies," the waiter came over and said. "Take your time and just let me know when you're ready to pay it." He placed it down on the table and walked away.

"I got it," I said, pulling the cash out of my purse. They both looked at me like, "Really?"

"Are you sure?" Libbe asked. "Girl, we ate everything on the menu."

"Yes, I'm sure. It's all on me this time," I insisted.

Libbe looked to Jackie and said, "In that case, I'll have another glass of champagne, please."

We all let out a laugh.

One thing I will say about my friends is that they are no slouches, so they know I wasn't trying to show off or flaunt. Libbe always had a fancy job, two sometimes. And I know Jackie was paid, because I was paying her. My mom and dad might not have given me a sister, but God blessed me with many. The three of us loved each other genuinely. We were the type of group to be out shopping individually and see something that we knew the other would like or look fabulous in and buy it for them just because.

If I've said it once, I've said it a thousand times. If I had, then my peoples had. And what I now had was a record deal, which meant I had a lot!

Chapter 10

The G-Unit camp and I were in Finland. We had just finished a sold out show. Afterward we headed back to the hotel. My security, Damon, and road manager, Andre—who we called Pretty Sha—always walked me back to my room. Pretty Sha was just outright hilarious. We joked around more than Paul and I ever did. After this particular show, and after walking me to my hotel room, Sha came back a few minutes later, pounding on my door like he was either the police or coming to let me know there was a fire and I needed to evacuate.

"Yo, Liv," he called while simultaneously knocking. "Oh, Livy Liv!"

"What's up?" I called out, making my way over to the door. I flung the door open. "What's up?" I'm looking over his shoulder for the po-po or the damn fire.

"I'm just sayin'," he started. "We tryna knock something down, but shorty say she wanna knock you down too, ya heard?"

At this point, I just started cracking up. He was talking all that slang and with extra hand movement. "Sha, what the hell are you talking about?" This dude was like on about ten he was so amped up. Sha always talked liked he was fast-talking somebody or he was pimpin'! Ol' Katt Williams—ass Negro. I can't.

"I'm saying, Ma, shorty wanna get with you, so I'm gon' tell her, 'Okay, we'll let you meet Liv, but you gotta see us first.' You feel me?" Sha winked and then let out this mischievous laugh.

I was still dying laughing at this point. Now, I know Sha just wanted me to act like I was going to be in on this little joke of theirs, but that shit would never happen in a million years. Oh my gosh, he drove me crazy with his shenanigans. He always had some type of joke he was playing on somebody or scheming on something. I could count on Sha for a good laugh at any time of the day. He was just a fun-loving guy. We all liked Pretty Sha. He didn't mean any harm and would never try to insult me. He was just crazy as hell . . . and obviously horny on tours!

"Easy, killer. Y'all are the worst. Yo, you know I ain't with none of that shit. I got nothing against what y'all do, but Liv don't get down with the females . . . not even so you can get some. Now, I'll play along with meeting the chick, but that's it. So whatever y'all tryna do to get shorty, just hurry up, because I'm about to eat this dessert tray I got in here then tap out."

"Man, we know you ain't wit' all that. Easy, killer. I got you, mama," he said as he was mocking me and busted out in laughter. "We just gon' let her believe she gon' get wit' you. You know how we do, boo. Gotta give the bitches hope sometimes. I'ma be right back."

He walked off with his pants sagging, doing the funniest George Jefferson walk ever. I just shook my head laughing and went back over to enjoy some of the goodies on my dessert tray. Man, I would be dreaming about getting back to my room after a show to that dessert tray. I may be small, but I love a good cheesecake and chocolate-covered strawberries. Our tour chef knew that was my guilty pleasure and that I always had to have it after a show. The dudes would have groupies waiting on them in their rooms, but I had desserts waiting to be devoured in mine.

About five minutes later, Sha was back knocking at my door. I could hear his laugh from the other side before

I even got to the door. I rolled my eyes up in my head. "Here we go." I opened the door, and Sha was there with his lady friend who wanted to get her paws on me. She was petite, very blonde, and very excited. Ol' girl was standing at my door shocked once she saw it was me who'd answered the door.

She was smiling from ear to ear, and then she got to babbling and rambling on. She didn't speak good English at all either. I don't even know how Sha managed to negotiate a deal with her in the first place. I couldn't understand a word that was coming out of her mouth. But then again, his ass was barely speaking good English himself with all his slang.

The chick was stuttering and just giddy as hell. Plus, she might have been a little full off of liquor the way she kept rambling, and I hadn't said one word back. I just had that stupid, lame grin on. You know the one you do when your friends embarrass you out in public. I had to finally say something.

"Hi, darling." I waved to her as I stood there in my fluffy white hotel robe. I then gave Sha a look that said, "What now? 'Cause y'all ain't coming up in here."

Sha said to the girl, "See, you see Olivia is here. Now you come back with me and then we can talk about Olivia." He was talking loud and using his hands and stuff to express his words. It was crazy. Why is it that when some people are speaking to someone who doesn't speak or understand English, they speak loud, point, and act out the words?

I just shook my head and shut the door, laughing all the way back over to my cheesecake. That damn girl had no idea what she was about to get herself into, but I'm sure she didn't mind. Those girls knew what they were doing, just sitting in the hotel lobby waiting for us to get back. Tuh, the stuff I saw on the regular was just crazy, but I don't think I'd ever seen anything crazier than 50's episode with a certain Miss Goody Two-Shoes turned housewife.

There was this one famous Hollywood actress 50 was smashing, seeing, dating; I don't know what to call it. She was a cool girl, pretty, young, booked a lot of good movies, so to see her act a flippin' fool over 50, some gangster rapper who she knew had broads at his hotel room whenever he wanted, was just crazy. Why do we women think we are always going to be the exception?

I will never, and I mean never, forget her laying out on the hotel lobby floor, throwing a tantrum like a bad-ass kid in the supermarket. I didn't know whether to feel sorry for her and pick her up off the floor, or be embarrassed and keep my head down and walk away.

"Come on, let's go," 50 said to all of us.

I believe we were about to head out to make an appearance at a club or something, and I think that's why ol' girl was tripping. She didn't want 50 to go and leave her at the hotel. He didn't want her to go, and told her to just wait at the hotel for him. The details of what started the scene are unclear, but her grown ass sprawled out on the floor in the hotel lobby, kicking, screaming, crying, and cussing is one hundred percent clear.

"Yo, Fif," I said, then eyeballed her on the ground while discretely double-nodding my head her way. I gave him a look like, "What about her?"

"I said let's go," he reiterated. "Leave her ass right there."

The rest of us looked at each other. Banks, Buck, and I had to keep it moving. She wasn't our girl. We shrugged our shoulders and then one by one walked over and around her like she was trash on the sidewalk. If that wasn't some classic *New Jack City* shit . . . I know to this day she wished she hadn't given 50 her nookie.

My cousin Jackie, who traveled with me as my assistant, always had stories about the guys to look forward to in the morning. She was on almost every tour with us. The only time she missed tours was when it was just 50 Cent and me on the road. I didn't need her then because it was just us and our stylist. Those were the most peaceful dates, the ones without the guys and their entourages running around the hotel. Jackie would have loved Brazil. I'm so grateful I got to visit the most beautiful places in the world and got paid to do it!

The full G-Unit tour was usually about fifteen of us. Unless we were doing a solo tour, which was just me, Banks, Buck and 50 Cent. Yayo couldn't accompany us to certain countries because of his criminal past. 50 Cent had signed all the hottest rappers at one point. There was Mobb Deep, M.O.P, Mase, Young Buck, Lloyd Banks, Yayo and myself. We all had our own tour buses—well, the principals did, which was me, Banks, Buck, Yayo and 50.

Banks' and Buck's bus always smelled like Amsterdam. Meanwhile, mine was obviously the girlie bus. I had candles, goodies, games, snacks, and healthy food. The guys were always tryna steal something off my bus because I had all the good stuff.

I'll never forget Pretty Sha and 50 Cent's road manager, Hov, coming on my bus and seeing my whole Jamaican food section. Cousin Jackie never left home without Jamaican essentials. Thank God for that, because I rarely ate fast food on the tours unless we had no other choice.

"Bumba clot, Jackie. Where you find Milo?"

"Gal, you know mi pack up di suitcase wit' nuff tings before we did pull out," Jackie boasted.

"Corn beef and hard dough bread. Lawd God, you even pack di condense milk. Woooy let me mek some Milo right now."

Jackie looked at Hov and Sha. In their worst Jamaican accents, which sounded like a mix of Irish and Haitian, they said, "We wan' sum too."

Man, that was the funniest. Them cats were as serious as a heart attack! We had to give them some Jamaican delicacies off their efforts alone. Jackie unpacked all of her stash and spread everything out over the counter.

"Sha, don't you go telling anybody we have di good good yardie food deh yah or unu cut off," I told him. Translated: "Don't tell anyone we have good Jamaican food or you guys won't get anymore."

"Man, we ain't tryna mess this up," Sha said. "I'm tired of eating Mickey D's with them fools, ya heard."

Once I'd been found out, every chance they got, them fools came by my bus to see what we were cooking. I had the large George Foreman grill on my bus too. We thought of everything.

I think the funniest time on my tour bus was when Mase came by one afternoon. That guy is hilarious. Well, he chose the wrong time to stop by this day.

See, Jackie loooooves Jamaican cheese, but it doesn't quite agree with her stomach. So she was letting out some mean silent farts on my bus. Oh my God, the shit was hilarious. Mase walked in and immediately said, "Aw, damn! Jackie got the bus smelling like warm poop."

You had to be there to know how funny that was. Mase already talks a bit slow. He's very smart, just talks slow—that's my waiver so that folks don't think I'm trying to call him retarded. I know how y'all try to twist stuff around.

One of the sweetest guys on the tour had to be Havoc from Mobb Deep. Havoc was never really talkative with me, but always pleasant. One night after a show, I went back to my hotel room and there was a big bouquet of red roses waiting for me. I looked on the card, and to my surprise it was from Havoc's quiet self. The card said something about me being beautiful. I guess he had a little crush on me, but he never once tried to make a move. He was always a gentleman in front of me.

Lloyd Banks was probably the coolest one on the tour with me besides 50 Cent. Young Buck and I always had a weird relationship. We never really hung out or spoke; just the cordial hello and good-byes when we saw each other. One night on tour, Buck and I locked eyes on stage. It was one of those double-take kind of things. I found myself wondering, *Do I got a thing for Buck?*

Back then I kind of dug thugged-out guys—call it my Tupac phase—but I was never one to have a "type" of guy I liked. I always thought Buck was a handsome, chocolate brother, but before that night, talking to him had never crossed my mind. We finally started to have a friendship and began talking on the phone. Buck had gotten my phone number from Pretty Sha and took the initiative to reach out to me first.

For the next few weeks, anytime we had a show Buck would bring me out on stage and we would both blush at each other or do one another's adlibs sometimes. It was so cute and crazy. It had sparked out of nowhere it seemed.

Even if we crossed one another on stage, we couldn't help but stare at each other for a few seconds. No one ever teased us or called us out on it either. I don't know how people couldn't tell we were starting to like each other. I just think they thought we were putting on a show. But it was no show. We were actually feeling each other.

We had all flown to Miami for a huge show. I think we bought out half the hotel we stayed at. What I didn't know was there was a surprise gift waiting for me in my suite.

I walked in my hotel room, dropped my bags, and checked out the fabulous suite. The room was set up like a beachfront bungalow. White décor was everywhere, with splashes of teal and sea shells and starfish as accents. I went to the back, and there sprawled out on the bed, fully clothed might I add, was Shaggy, arms folded behind his head with a smirk on his face.

I had been kicking it with reggae singer Shaggy off and on. We knew each other in the industry and had connected to do some work together. I'd had my first meeting with him at his ranch in Long Island with my cousin Paul back in the day. We discussed doing a record together and how I could bust more into my roots with reggae music and features. As Shaggy spoke to me, I often drifted back in time to when the "Mr. Boombastic" video came out on *Video Music Box* and I would watch him as a teenager. I would boggle and whine to that video so hard in my parents' living room. If my mom ever caught me she would probably punish me for dancing so vulgar!

It was crazy that one day I found myself in his house talking business. One time I went over to his house by myself to use the studio he had built in the basement. After the session he walked me outside, and we leaned up on my car and just shot the breeze for a little while.

I don't even know how I got on the subject, but I remember telling him that I had a crush on him back in the day. I felt like a little schoolgirl with a crush on her math teacher or something. See, Shaggy was thirteen years older than me, but he was very handsome and charismatic. I didn't even see age. I just saw a man in good shape and someone who made me laugh and smile.

His reply to me was, "Aw, baby girl, you couldn't handle a bad man like me."

Licking my lips and raising my eyebrow, being all grown, I looked him up and down and said, "Hmm, I guess I'll take my chances."

From that day on, Shaggy's and my relationship went from business to a wild rollercoaster ride that should have had a warning sign posted on it. "Ride at your own risk. "May bump your head a few times. May fall off ride."

We'd only been kicking it for a couple of months when Shaggy decided to take it upon himself and come to the G-Unit tour in Miami. He hadn't called, given me the heads up or anything. Now, if he had been my *man*—like steady relationship—the shit would have been all good, but that wasn't the case with me and Shaggy. Like I said, we were just kickin' it. He called himself pulling that let-me-sneak-up-on-her mess because he really didn't know what was going on while I was touring with all these rappers.

"Surprise, honey!" he yelled

"Oh, shit." I placed my hand on my chest. "How the hell did you get in here, and why wasn't I informed you were coming?" I feigned being perturbed and then laughed and went and jumped on the bed and kissed him. Yeah, I was feeling a certain kind of way about his no-call, but a part of me was happy to see him. "Nice surprise, though, wit' yo' sneaky ass. How did you even get in here?"

"You can't hide from me. Girl, you are mine," he said, kissing me back. "I always know how to find you."

Smug bastard!

I didn't know if I liked that he was so confident, because even though I didn't want to admit it then, I was catching feelings for Shaggy! Ugh!

He rose up from the bed. "Let's go have a drink, babes. Put on your two-piece so we can go hang by the pool." He was hugging all over me like I needed a bribe for a drink and the pool. I dug in my bag for my two-piece bikini and cover up.

"Sure, let me go freshen up and then we are outta here, papa."

So, I put on my suit and we headed out to the elevators so that we could go down to the pool. I always requested on tour that my room be in a different wing of the hotel from the other artists because I liked the peace and quiet. Besides that, I didn't want to have to walk out of that door and see their groupies lined up in the hallway. I didn't expect to run into anybody as we waited for the elevator. But when Shaggy and I were standing there waiting, being all mushy, hugged up and kissing on one another, the elevator door opened and BOOM! It was 50 Cent, Buck, and Yayo. I wished that at that very moment I was invisible. Like, why couldn't I have had Dorothy's red ruby slippers on and be back in Kansas?

"Aw, shit. Look what we got here," 50 Cent said. He seemed like he couldn't wait to grill me, so I went on and made the introductions before he could start clowning.

"Fif, this is Shaggy. Shaggy, this is Fif," I introduced.

They gave each other dap and pulled in for a man hug.

"Pleasure to meet you, fam," Shaggy said to 50 Cent. "I hope you been taking good care of my girl." He squeezed me in closer to him and kissed my forehead. He wasn't fooling anybody. He was just trying to make his mark.

At this point, Buck was friggin' pissed! I mean, he was mean-muggin'. I don't think he even said hello. He might have given Shaggy a head nod and then breezed right past me. Man, if looks could kill . . .

You would have thought something had actually gone down between Buck and me the way he was acting. Yeah, we had been crushing on each other and conversing on the phone, but that was the extent of it. We had never gotten physical or anything. I could see why he might have felt a little salty; I would have been a little pissed, too, if the tables had been turned, but Buck took being mad at me to a whole new level, though. I mean, all the other guys would just tease me and yell out, "Mr. Boombastic," when they saw me. Yayo would even joke and try to speak patois and do a bad Shaggy impersonation. But Buck—he stopped speaking to me altogether. There was no more locking eyes on stage. All I got was evil eyes. He didn't even walk to my side of the stage if we were on together. Sheesh! It got hella awkward. He took that shit so serious that we really stopped speaking period.

That right there taught me to never even almost try to kick it with somebody that was part of the crew ever again. Man, shit was stressful.

One thing I do miss about the Unit is that we used to always gather as a group at 50's mansion in Connecticut.

"I bought this place so we would have somewhere all of us can work and relax as a unit with no issues." He had that Tony Soprano boss talk down pact. "Whenever y'all want to do anything, you come here. If you need a vacay, come here. You need to record, come here. We need a spot to do a video shoot, we can do everything in-house. *Mi casa, su casa.* This is G-Unit's spot," 50 said.

We did end up shooting a couple of videos there. 50 planned several events there as well.

He was always on top of handling business. I admired his leadership, initiative, and passion. And yes, I must confess it was indeed very attractive.

We had huge G-Unit parties at the mansion. The press and the who's who in the industry were always invited. Actors, rappers, athletes, models—it was insane. Can you say *lavish*? At this one party we did, 50 went all out. We had an All-white Affair, meaning everyone had to dress in white. He turned the mansion into Pee Wee's Playhouse, Hefner's Playboy bunny mansion, and the best industry party I had ever been to in my life! He had swings installed in one room for models in lingerie to swing on. A mural painted of me, Banks, Buck, and him was in one of the many foyers. There were professional masseuses and tattoo artists on hand, drinks and food flowing with waiters at every corner, and entertainment in every room. It was so overwhelming, but I loved it!

On the weekends all of us would gather at 50's house. 50 had bought us all ATVs and had a trail built around his house. We absolutely loved those things. I rode mine every weekend. My tomboy ways never changed. One of the boys until the day I die; that's why I didn't have many fears when it came to being brought into G-Unit, which was absolutely male dominated. I loved them like family. We argued, made up, fought, partied, and broke bread as a family.

It was really good times. One time at the mansion after dinner, 50 and I had one of our private talks. We would often have deep conversations about any and everything. 50's intelligence made him attractive. Listening to a man speak, especially a smart man, made him appealing. We spent quality time with one another on and off tour. That alone can make you have a growing attraction for someone.

"Look, I think you are a beautiful woman, very smart and talented, so I would be lying if I said I wasn't attracted to you," he told me. "But we can never cross that line, because I think it will ruin everything. There is far too much money to be made, and besides, I know you ain't that type of chick. I have a lot of respect for you, so I wouldn't even do you like that. If you and I started messing around, we'd never be able to convince the rest of the world that we are not." 50 absolutely approached the situation like a boss.

As I listened to him speak, it made me just that much more attracted to him! Damn. But what he was speaking was the truth.

"Well, Fif, I'm not going to lie and say the feeling isn't mutual, but I agree. Crossing that line would be detrimental. I look up to you way too much to ruin what we have. I can talk to you about anything and never once worry about being judged. You have given me great advice since day one and treated me like a princess always. I'm just glad we got that out the way and we can keep it moving with no awkwardness between us." I let out a sigh of relief after getting all that out.

"A'ight." He smiled and then laughed that distinctive laugh that we all know and love so much.

After that, it was much easier to have conversations about people who liked us. Man, we would tease each other like big kids. Looking back, I honestly can't imagine it being any other way. I actually miss being able to call 50 and get some advice. Street dude or not, he was definitely wise.

50 and I never had to revisit that conversation again. We knew what it was and left it right there.

Chapter 11

Trust me, I learned a lot, to say the least, while rolling on tour with G-Unit. I met some other great people as a result of my connection to G-Unit. There was one person in particular that I reconnected with that I'd originally met on a video shoot.

We were shooting Tony Yayo's video for the song "Curious." Denyce Lawton was the leading lady. Denyce has since played on Tyler Perry's *House of Payne*, but back then she'd done music videos such as "The Way" by Clay Aiken, "Peaches & Cream" by 112, "One Mic" by Nas, and "Anything" by Jaheim. Denyce and I became cool after that video experience, but things got so heated on set, our relationship could have gone either way. Because of the drama that happened that day, I could have easily turned out to be her enemy.

"Hey, Liv, I want you to meet somebody real quick," said Misa Hylton, Puffy's baby mama, who was the stylist for the shoot. Misa went over and tapped on the shoulder of this girl who was sitting on set chopping it up with Yayo before the shoot got started. The rest of the crew hadn't arrived yet. As a matter of fact, we were waiting on them to get things poppin'.

Misa walked back over to me with this beautiful black and Korean girl. I could definitely see why she was chosen to be the leading lady. She was no background extra.

"Liv, this is Denyce. Denyce, this is Olivia," Misa introduced.

The two of us shook hands and immediately began talking.

"It's so crazy to meet you," Denyce said. "I was already a fan of your voice. Girl, you need a solo album."

"Thank you," I replied.

"So, how do you like G-Unit?" Denyce asked.

"It's been dope. The guys are great," I said.

Misa excused herself to go take care of some business. Denyce and I continued chatting like old friends.

"Yeah, the guys seem pretty cool." She looked over at Yayo. "At least Marvin is anyway." Marvin is Yayo's given name. "I've been sitting over there talking to Yayo. He is so sweet." I saw her cheeks get a li'l flushed.

"Yeah, y'all been chillin' for a minute." I play-hit her on the shoulder. "I see you, boo boo." I winked.

She laughed. "Girl, stop. He ain't even my type. I'm just saying he's sweet. For real, he is a really nice guy. He's been telling me all about his daughter and how he wants to get Lasik eye surgery. He's a down to earth guy."

"Okay, okay, calm down. I'm just messing with you. But yeah, he's good peoples." I smirked.

"Yo, yo, yo! Let's get this party started," I heard.

I turned to see the rest of the G-Unit crew coming in, eyes glazed, and reeking of weed, of course.

"Okay, well, it looks like it's about time to set it off. Let me go have Misa finish getting me together," I said. On my way to get with Misa, I ran into Lloyd so I stopped for a minute just to see what was up with him.

"Fuck you, bitch!"

Both Lloyd and I turned to see what was going on; why all of a sudden someone was going off.

"Fuck you too. You ain't shit." I saw Denyce snapping off at Yayo. "Never in my life of doing videos have I ever been so disrespected or felt so uncomfortable. This is bullshit!"

Denyce gathered her things and headed straight for the exit.

"Whoa, whoa, hold up," Gil Green, the director of the video said as he tried to calm Denyce down and get her to stay and do the shoot. She was not having it.

"Hell, no. I didn't even want to do this damn video in the first place. But 50 and Misa persuaded me into it by saying"—imitating 50 Cent—"Yo, ma, Yayo is a big fan of yours ever since he was locked up. He had ya posters hanging in his jail cell."

All the guys started riffing and laughing at Yayo. "Oh, Yayo got a little crush," someone teased.

"Man, I ain't thinking about that ho. We can get any bad bitch to do this shoot. Fuck her. Let her ass leave and call the next one in line."

"Yeah, y'all do that shit, 'cause this bad bitch ain't being in shit." Denyce was on fire. Her determination to get up out of there was more than evident.

"Come on now, Denyce. He just got a li'l hype 'cause the fellas walked in and he didn't wanna look soft in front of them. He lost his cool. Please don't take it personal. It's true; he is a fan of yours. The first thing he said when he got the treatment was that he wanted that girl from Jaheim's video," Gil pleaded. He then looked over at me and shot me a look that said, "Come on, Olivia. Help a brotha out."

I guess because I was the only other sensible female there, he felt that she could probably relate to me better. He wanted me to have a little one on one with her to get her to change her mind. I didn't necessarily want to try to get her to stay, because Yayo was absolutely out of line and being rude as hell. I did feel bad and wanted to let her know I wasn't with that type of ignorant mess. The last thing I wanted her to do was to think I was cut from the same cloth.

By the time I decided to try to talk with her and get her to come back and do the shoot, she was headed off set. There was this whizzing sound and then a crashing sound. Yayo's ass had thrown a bottle at this girl.

"Oh, she's definitely not coming back," I said out loud.

"Oh, hell no!" Denyce yelled as she tried to charge back toward Yayo and his crew that was pumping him up by laughing at his actions.

That's when Lloyd and I went after Denyce and helped get her out of there.

"Come on. Let's just go sit down for a minute so you can calm down," I said as Lloyd and I took her into one of the trailers.

Lloyd got her something to drink while I sat down next to her on the couch.

"I don't know what just happened out there, but Yayo was definitely outta character," I told her. "Don't let no childish dudes stop you from getting your paper." I looked her up and down. "You're here now. You aren't doing this for Yayo. You are doing this to broaden your reel and get more gigs. Snatch this paper up and then be out." I was trying my best to help Gil Green out, but shit, I wasn't believable to myself. I would have left too! Threw up my middle finger and never looked back.

She rolled her eyes and shook her head. "I should have gone on with my better judgment and turned this gig down. I don't even know why I let 50 and Misa gas me up like that just for me to come here and be treated like some bird bitch. Uh-uh."

Lloyd and I looked at each other. We did not want to be labeled and clumped into the same category as that buffoonery that had just taken place. Denyce must have seen the expressions on our faces.

"No, not you two. Y'all are cool people. 50 is a nice guy too. I know if he was out there he would have shut that shit down. But Marvin, aka Yayo, and them other minions, they are fucking whack!"

"I don't understand. You were just saying how nice Yayo was."

"That was until Young Buck and all them other niggas showed up. Then he just started fronting. We were rehearsing a scene of the video. I had even gotten him to smile and laugh against his will, because he was trying to be all hard. Then those guys show up and . . ." She was so upset that she couldn't even finish.

I was sitting there with Lloyd like, "Damn, we can't even blame her for not wanting to do the shoot." But we had a video to shoot, and we weren't about to let Yayo's crazy ass mess up our paper either.

We did end up convincing Denyce to go ahead and do the shoot and get it over with.

That video was almost never aired because Denyce was so pissed it took her a month to even sign the release papers. When I tell you this was the ghetto version of that scene in the movie *Grease,* where Danny gets around all his boys and then tries to front on Sandy . . . Just madness.

But no matter what, G-Unit was still my fam, and even though it was a golden opportunity to work with them all, in the back of my mind I was always anxious to work on my own solo album.

Once we finally did focus on my solo project, it was time to figure out how 50 was going to market me. He was so selfless that he used me on his first single entitled "Candy Shop" to reintroduce me to the world. Neither of us had any idea it would be this number one single that sat at the top of the charts for over eight weeks straight.

I would thank God every day for such a great blessing. We were touring places outside of the country that I never dreamed I would see. Israel, Australia, Monaco, Thailand: you name it and we've been there.

One of the sweetest feelings had to be when we were in Venice, Italy. I was walking over a little overpass bridge and one of the guys who row people on the Gondolas spotted me and my hair/makeup guy and started singing "Candy Shop." I was floored! To be in such a faraway country and have people recognize me and sing my songs was such a priceless feeling. I'd never experienced anything like it.

"This is it!" I remember saying out loud to myself on my hotel balcony. "I have finally made it!" I was feeling like Eddie Murphy on his balcony in the movie *Coming to America*. I was just so damn happy in that moment. I was ready to head back into the studio, but this time I wanted to show the world what I was really made of.

"50, I want to do another record that showcases I can really sing," I told him once we were back in the States. "I mean, 'Candy Shop' is great, but I need to hit them with real vocals."

50 Cent laughed. "I hear you, but you see my plan is working, right?"

I nodded. I couldn't deny it. He was right; it was working thus far. I was international, for goodness' sake.

"They just need a li'l bit of O, and then throw me on the track, and then *bam!* You got a smash. Boo-yahhhh!"

"You are something else, Fif. I know you make shit hot—yeah, yeah, yeah—but the next record I gotta kill 'em on," I said. "The people are probably thinking I'm just in the group to sing on hooks, and that's not what I do. There is so much more to me than that."

"I know, Liv," he cosigned.

"Yeah, but the rest of the world doesn't."

Feeling empathy for where I was coming from, 50 once again put aside the hardcore record he was going to do so he could do another record with me. He was on a big wave from doing his new movie, *Get Rich or Die Trying*. He had a single off the movie soundtrack called "Best Friend."

Shaggy and I were now exclusive, so he was always around and checking in on me more often these days. When we shot the video for his song "wild 2nite" featuring me. He was checking on me in my trailor ever so often. My hair/makeup stylist Ray asked if he wanted his makeup done he kept coming in here so much. Shaggy was a clown and just liked to come mess with me. Director X did a great job on that video by the way. Anyway, we were chilling at Shaggy's crib one night and I was coming out of the bathroom when I got a call from 50.

"Wassup, baby?" 50 said, sounding all excited, like he had a secret and couldn't wait to tell me.

"Whaddup, boo boo? You back in town?" I asked him. Boo boo was 50's nickname in the hood.

"Yeah, I'm back. I need you to cut this record. I want you on the remix for 'Best friend.'"

My musical antenna shot straight up. "Man, hell yeah. I can write my parts right now," I told him. "I'm at Shaggy's and he got a studio in the crib. I got you. Done deal. I'll send you back the vocals tomorrow."

"A'ight, bet. Don't fuck this up now," he said with a laugh and then we both hung up.

As soon as I ended the call, I grabbed a pad and started jotting down my verse ideas. I was so hype; I wanted to tell Shaggy the good news. I ran downstairs to the basement, where he had just happened to be in the booth working on something himself.

In patois I called out to him, "Bwoy, come outta di booth. I got another one." I was sliding around the studio on the hardwood floors like I did back when I was a little girl in my mother's kitchen. "I got another hot joint 50 wants me to be on."

He came out of the booth smiling. "What's up, babes? Why you so rass happy?" he asked, which meant why was I so damn happy.

"I said I got another hot joint 50 wants me to be on. I just spoke to him and he wants me on the remix of the

'Best Friend' record he got off of his movie soundtrack. He's going to push it as a single."

"Aw, shit! You betta make my money, baby." Did I mention Shaggy was the little comedian too?

I smirked at him. "Boy, cut di fuckery," I said, which meant for him to stop playing.

I spent a couple of hours laying the vocals so that I could have them to 50 by morning just as promised. In a matter of time, history was repeating itself. We had yet another number one record. We couldn't lose. More touring followed. There were private jets, private catering, wardrobe and hairstylist on the road with us, all day every day. Things couldn't be better, right? That's what one would think. That's what I thought at first. I mean, here I was doing all this work—yet I felt like I'd had more money in my bank account when I was working at BBH!

When I questioned the label about why I was touring all over the place but wasn't getting any checks for that, I was told that, in my case, it was just a promo tour. Translated: I was doing all this work for free just to get my name out there.

I still don't understand that to this day. Fans were paying money for tickets to the shows to see the acts. I was part of the act, which in essence means they were paying to see me. I'm not saying that they were paying just to see me, but what few who were, that still should equal out to some money, right? One would think that anyway.

When it came to paperwork and contracts for touring, I didn't have to sign additional paperwork, because I was signed to both G-Unit and Violator, so Lighty was supposed to have me covered. The manager signs off on tour paperwork. I didn't question the money because it was always coming in.

When I found out how much Buck and Banks were being paid for a promo tour, that's when I lost it. How the fuck they getting paid for promo but I'm not?

Now I get that Banks had his "Hunger for More" album out and Buck had "Cashville," but still, I was due something. Granted my album wasn't out, but I was still putting in the same hard work and dedication as they were. I was getting chump change compared to them.

On top of that, I still hadn't received any money from the "Candy Shop" record or all the ringtone money we made off the song. So I was not being paid properly, nor was I getting the credit I deserved as a solo artist. Everything was adding up, but my shit was coming up negative.

In all honesty, up until that point I really hadn't been able to show that I could sing. In the beginning I would only come out and do hooks. Then 50 started letting me perform full songs during our set. That fact bothers me the most, because for a while people didn't know I had the powerhouse voice that I possess. People still weren't seeing me as the true R&B artist that I was. I take that very seriously. True artists are sensitive about their craft. In the words of Erykah Badu, "I'm an artist, and I'm sensitive about my shit."

Perhaps because I had started asking questions, eventually money was coming in, but it still wasn't what I should have been making for sure. I hadn't gotten a royalty check for writing and laying vocals on "Candy Shop" or "Best Friend." It was starting to dawn on me that maybe it was a conflict of interest to have Chris Lighty managing me, because he was also 50's manager, and 50 was my boss. But fair is fair, right? Not so much!

I was not being paid properly—period! Of course, I asked about my money every chance I got, but I always got the run around.

"Yeah, we're looking into it."

"We put in a claim."

"I'm working on it."

Different day, same shit, was all I kept hearing.

In addition to not being paid for what I'd done on "Candy Shop" and "Best Friend," neither of those songs still allowed me to show what I was made of vocally. Let's be clear; they were great records. They were radio-friendly records that followed 50's strategy, but no matter how you looked at it, to some people, I was just some chick singing hooks.

50 wanted me to do records that fit the G-Unit brand, not Olivia the solo R&B singer–type records. It was always a hook here and a hook there, everywhere a hook-hook! And when 50 did pick records, it was something I didn't want to go with. We never argued about records, but I always voiced my opinion on what songs I thought should be the single to release and not what he chose. He kept choosing records I did for mix tapes, which were meant for play, in my opinion. But 50 always gets the last word, so my opinion went unheard.

"So, when can we go with something I actually approve of as my single?" I said. "How many times do I have to sing a hook or put out a rap record? Your prototype doesn't work for me, Fif." I was overwhelmed with frustration, but we were still having a level-headed conversation.

"Look, Liv, I know you want to get your stuff out, but I'm telling you I really know what I'm doing," 50 told me. "We are going to continue to tour overseas and promote the songs we have out now; then we can talk about putting your album out when we're done with all that, okay?"

I looked at him. "That's going to be a whole other issue, 'cause you will probably tell me my songs I chose to make the album don't fit your plan," I said sarcastically. "Or who knows how long we are going to be on tour for? It may be another year before you put my album out. We need time to promote my singles. If I'm overseas with y'all, how am I going to promote my stuff?" I had so many concerns that I constantly voiced.

50 and I spoke about this many times. We had tons of conversations where I asked him to have Jimmy Iovine let me out of my Interscope contract, but 50 would always

say, "Nah, we gon' work this out. I'm going to make sure it works."

I trusted him, and I just knew he would be able to fix it. Turns out it just wasn't something we could work out, so eventually I made the hard decision that I had to split from G-Unit. Before I could even have the final conversation with Fif, my friend Laurie, who was Lighty's executive assistant, called to give me a heads-up.

"Hey, Liv," Laurie said.

"Hey, mama, what's up?" I replied.

Kind of hesitant, Laurie said, "I'm not even supposed to be telling you this, but they are letting you out of your contract and releasing you from G-Unit."

Hearing her words was a complete shock. I had been asking for almost two years to get out of my contract. I just wasn't seeing the advantage of being at that label anymore. So what had changed now? Why would he choose so abruptly to let me go? And why couldn't he call and tell me this himself? I wasn't upset as much as I was confused. Why now?

I didn't trip or go fishing and picking Laurie for more answers. I just paused and then hit Laurie with a plain and simple, "Okay."

"Are you sure everything is okay?" Laurie asked.

"Yup, and thanks for telling me, mama." I hung up.

My thoughts were moving a mile a minute, because in true hustler fashion, I was already thinking about the next step and how I could finally get my solo career back up and running. There was no time to keep questioning things or to be disappointed like when I was released from J Records. I had actually wanted out of this one.

When you are a child of God, you don't wallow and depress yourself. I give God thanks no matter the situation, because He will always bring bigger and better. Don't settle for less when God has made you for more.

He has always brought me through it. I'd already gotten two record deals, so there was never any doubt that there would be a third one.

I said, "Lord, this third deal is going to be the one that takes me there. I will just wait on you." And just like that, I kept it moving.

There are people who can't even get one deal, so I was not taking any of my opportunities for granted. If I could do it once, I could always do it again . . . only in a better situation next time, no riding on anybody's coattails with the chances of falling off.

I don't know if I was relieved or upset that 50 hadn't called me himself to tell me the news. I even wondered if they had put Laurie up to calling me so that they wouldn't have to. Nah, because that would have made them cowards, right?

The following week, I received the termination paperwork from my lawyer. I don't remember how the conversation happened, but it was a relief to be away from the drama. I still had plenty of upcoming shows and money in the bank.

I didn't have a conversation with 50 until maybe two years later. Real talk. I happened to bump into him outside of JFK Airport, and it was kind of awkward. However, we hugged briefly and he told me to call him next week when he returned from his trip.

Sometimes I could not read him. He was so hot and cold. I have seen him full of emotion, kind and generous, and I have seen him emotionless, cold-hearted and nonchalant. He's like the wind. You never know which way he's going to go.

I will always be grateful to Fif and will never have any love loss. Sometimes things just don't work out the way you expect them to.

A few weeks after they announced I had been dropped from G-Unit, I was already back on tour overseas. It was very weird at times, because I had one tour in particular with Banks in Korea, and they were still announcing me as Olivia from G-Unit. It was rough because everything was so fresh, and I had to go and perform all those songs like I was happy about how shit turned out. I was fucking annoyed. I was tired of questioning my talent.

"Man, I know I'm the shit," I would fuss at myself/ give myself a pep talk. "I can sing a capella on cue, dance, and I write my own music. I just don't get it. Why do I keep getting into deals that don't let me show my true artistry?" It hurt knowing that I couldn't do shit about certain things. But one thing was for certain: I always got a deal!

When I got back home from tour it was still bad, because whenever I did shows, interviews, or whatever, people would introduce me as "Olivia, formerly of G-Unit." Do you even understand how annoying that became? I'd be cringing with my insides shouting, *Just announce me as Olivia! Damn!*

I was always putting trust into people in this industry. I didn't understand why this kept happening to me. Here I was again, for the second time, with no label to back me. Even though this is what I wanted, to be a solo artist, I didn't want to be one without a label. "God, what am I doing wrong?" I shouted, punching down hard on the couch.

The second time being let go from a label, I took the fall hard. I questioned myself every day on why I even went to G-Unit in the first place. Why did they even choose me to be in the group? Was there something I was missing in God's plan? Why wasn't anything working out? One minute I was high on the mountaintops in Greece or on luxurious hotel balconies in Monaco, and then the next thing I knew, I was back in the valley—literally, because I was living in L.A. at the time.

I couldn't help but think that maybe this was God's way of saying, "You were always handed things, Olivia. Now you need to experience how it feels to have things taken away." But I always worked my butt off to get where I was. My talent was what got me those things and let me experience those places. Is that how God really works? Does He give you things only to take them away? I never questioned God, but I did start to question my faith.

From that moment on, I made a conscious decision to not give a damn about the way everybody wanted me to do things. Nobody else's way had worked out, as far as I was concerned. Next time, I was going to do things my way. I was going to work harder than before and get my hands all the way dirty to prove that this was what I wanted. I was going to fight for the things I wanted in life, and although things might have been taking a little longer than expected, the reward in the end would be so much sweeter. It just had to be. I was going to run my own race and not worry about what was going on in someone else's lane.

I remembered that same teacher who had asked me about my passion in life also telling me that I should never give up on something I couldn't go a day without. For me, that something was music, so whatever obstacles I would have to overcome, I refused to allow them to hold me back.

It would be those invisible hurdles and the obstacles I never saw coming that would become the real problem.

Chapter 12

After the whole G-Unit fiasco, I decided to take some time to regroup and figure out my next move. I needed a plan, and giving up music was definitely not part of the plan. I just needed a moment to collect my thoughts. I had a lot of fans and supporters who were waiting on an album from me. I couldn't close down shop now.

It was now 2007, and I had so many offers for overseas dates still pouring in that I decided to do a few mini tours overseas. I had solo tours and spot dates with Lloyd Banks. I just needed to get away from all the G-Unit aftermath that was happening here in the States. What I mean by aftermath is that there were so many rumors flying around that I swear if I wasn't such a strong-willed individual I would have just lost it and jumped off a bridge.

For example, right after I got out of the meeting with Chris Lighty up at Violator, where we were discussing how we would handle my parting from G-Unit, I got in my car and peeled off down Thirty-fourth and Ninth. We had said we were going to come up with a plan that made everybody look good, but we didn't have anything solid yet. I turned on the radio and immediately recognized the voice of Wendy Williams. She mentioned that she had just gotten some breaking news. I tuned out the voices in my head to listen to hers. Perhaps hearing someone else's drama would make me forget about my own.

I turned the volume up and waited for Wendy to drop the bomb.

"This is just in, people: Olivia, the first lady of G-Unit, has been dropped. You heard me: fired, cut from the team, through . . . as in *finished*!"

At that point, all I heard was the sound of a boiling teapot that someone had left on the stove. I was steaming! I had to ask myself if I'd really heard her right. I was in the car with Paul and I told him I was headed over to that she-man's office. We was fi'nna get this bullshit straight right now. I listened to her continue to make her snappy little comments and jokes about the situation . . . about my life. Hateful bitches always gotta make up their own assumptions. Why not ask me what happened first? Or call Chris Lighty? That shit boils my rabbit.

But what really had me tripping was trying to figure out how this woman somehow got inside information that I had just been let go from G-Unit. Granted, it was the truth, but when she decided to add her own two cents and proceed with slandering me, that's when it got ugly. She could have dipped out after she said Olivia just got dropped. End scene, go to commercial, bitch!

"She probably was a whore throwing it to all the guys, and when they were done using her, they just let her go," Wendy said.

Word? That's how you feel? She went on and on, telling lies about me, until I was pissed enough to finally turn off the radio. I have hated that woman ever since that day, and I still do. Period. All right, I might not still hate her, but I still can't stand her. A real chick with clout could have gotten me on the phone and cleared the situation up real quick instead of popping off at the mouth with lies. And there lies the difference between Oprah and a wannabe. Her name shouldn't even be used in the same sentence as Oprah . . . Tuh!

I've asked God daily to change my heart, to help me to forgive that woman so I could just let it go. I'm still a work in progress, because I have forgiven a lot of people over the years, but Wendy Williams is not one of them. That sister had so much power on radio at one point, and she chose to lie and defame a lot of people, including me, for ratings. Wendy Williams is definitely not her sister's keeper.

"What the F—k!" I spat, slamming my fist against the steering wheel after I'd cut off that woman's voice. I hated that a rat had run to the wolves so fast. I owed it to my fans to be the one to share it. We'd just made the decision in the office on how I would relay the news to my fans. Who the hell could have leaked it to her that fast? I guess wherever there is mud, there is going to always be a pig slinging it. I was livid, to say the least, but again and as always, I had to be the bigger person and let that shit go. As much as I wanted to drive up there or pull out my cell and call that woman up on the radio, check the situation and then tell her where, how, and when to shove it, it just wasn't worth it to me. Besides, that's exactly what she wanted me to do. That was her goal, her mission, and why she got the ratings she did. She knew how to piss people off just enough where they would call into the show, going off and making fools of themselves. That was not going to be Olivia Longott.

Being let go from G-Unit had been hard enough. They were like family. I didn't even know what to say to them. I had to just keep telling myself that there was a reason why I wasn't supposed to fully prosper in that group, and I was determined to figure it out. What I did learn, though, was how truly strong I was throughout the whole process.

It was only because I always knew my self-worth. The morals my parents instilled in me as a little girl were some of the many things that helped me through. I had great friends who had known me ever since I was a teenager and always reminded me I was destined for greatness.

There was one friend in particular, Gabrielle. She was a hairstylist. I met her when I was fifteen years old. I was walking down Linden Boulevard as I always did after school, with my all-white, pink-nosed pit bull named Soca. One of my friends had a litter of pits, and I was lucky enough to nab one. Soca was a baby pit bull at this time, so it wasn't like I was walking down the street scaring off the whole neighborhood with some big ol' beast of a dog. She was so little and cute, my little Soca. I am West Indian, so it was only right that I named my dog after our style of music. And yes, I had a pit bull named Reggae, too, but that wasn't until a few years later. We ended up having eight pits because the parents had puppies. Thank the Lord we had a nice size backyard. I don't know how my parents let me keep all those puppies. I did, though, eventually give some of them away.

Anyway, Gabrielle worked at the same unisex hair salon where Alexis worked. I would pass by or stop inside there occasionally after school to see Alexis. I had seen Gabrielle around, but we didn't know one another. One day she came outside and stopped me.

"Excuse me. You walk past here almost every day with your stylish hairstyles, and I just wanted to tell you how adorable you and your dog are," Gabrielle said. "By the way, I'm Gabrielle, but you might have heard everybody around here call me Gabby."

"Thank you," I replied. Gabrielle was cute, and not too cute where she felt she couldn't throw another sister a compliment. I immediately liked that about her. "My name is Olivia, and this is Soca. I gotta keep the hair right because I have an image, and I'm going to be a singer. When I become famous, I gotta look right on the red carpet," I joked and we both laughed.

"So you sing for real?" she replied with an intrigued smile.

"Yup, and I'm going to hire you as my hairstylist when I'm on the road," I added, meaning every word, because you couldn't tell me I wasn't going to make it in the music business. Alexis was the bomb stylist, but being a celebrity stylist wasn't really something she strove to be. Doing hair wasn't really Alexis's passion. It was just something she was good at. Gabrielle, on the other hand, her eyes lit up when I even mentioned her being my personal stylist. I knew she would be cut out for it, because I had seen her work in the salon alongside Alexis. Alexis was the one who had gotten her the job in the first place.

Gabrielle and I said a few more words, exchanged numbers, and stayed friends from that day on. We lost contact a few times, but always managed to somehow reconnect, and just like I told Gabrielle, when I became famous, I sure enough kept my word and hired her as my hairstylist. Even after being dropped from both labels abruptly, Gabrielle was always there for me to talk me through my depressed moments. I could always count on her for girl talk over wine or champagne to drown my troubles. She never wavered; instead, she always stood strong by my side. I only had a handful of real friends, and she was most certainly in my top five.

She is still one of my close friends to this day. I don't know what I would have done without her. Gabrielle truly is my sister. She was there for me when I was at my highest and at my lowest, always reminding me that God doesn't make mistakes and to keep pushing, because my blessing was right around the corner.

One night, Gabrielle and I were having drinks at her house when we got into one of our little conversations.

"Hey, sis, let me ask you a question?" I asked her.

Gabrielle replied eagerly, "Of course. Wassup?"

"Do you think I have what it takes to make it in this business? I mean really have what it takes?"

Gabrielle looked me straight in the eyes and then put down her drink. "Bitch, don't make me smack you."

I swear we must have laughed for about five minutes for sure, but then she got serious.

"You are absolutely amazing. Not only are you a great friend and godmother of my two kids, but you sing like nobody's business. You were born to do this. Don't let negativity and people who can't see how dope you are deter you from your dreams. They will catch up to you sooner or later. You are ahead of your time, Sissy. Believe that."

Just the sincerity in Gabrielle's eyes . . . her words . . . Before I knew it, tears were dripping into my drink. And it must have been contagious because I looked up and Gabrielle was sitting there crying too.

"Girl, stop it!" Gabrielle said while wiping her tears. "My makeup was fierce. Now you got me over here looking like a raccoon." With that our tears turned to laughter again.

Everyone needs a friend like Gabrielle. I was just so happy that I can be the same friend to her that she is to me. We go out of our way for each other and do things for one another just because. To me that is what true friendship really is: someone who can hold you down and lift you up, in the best and worst of times, without judgment. No matter how many times Gabby and I may have lost contact, we always came right back and picked up where we left off like we never separated in the first place. True friends don't have to speak to or see each other every day. Life gets busy, but it always comes back full circle.

Even with such a strong support system around me, I questioned myself a few times in this industry, always wondering why it seemed so much harder for women to get ahead in the game than it did for men. There always seemed to be those female artists whose singing was not half as good as mine, yet they somehow managed to get ahead. Well, I had slowly learned a few reasons why, thanks to 50.

Prior to my parting from G-Unit, 50 had taken me to a lot of dinner meetings and parties so that I would see and know how to conduct my own business affairs as shrewdly as he did. I saw and heard so many crazy things. One night in Beverly Hills we were meeting up with Jimmy Iovine and Ron Fair for a late dinner meeting. There was a girl on the Interscope label who used to be around way too much without her group. Usually you travel with your group members, right? At least that's how we always got down. So, when she was always flying around solo—like birds usually do, if you know what I mean—it set off a red flag in my head.

I honestly have no idea why she was putting herself out there like that trying to be seen. In all honesty, there were like five or six females in her group, and she automatically stood out amongst them all . . . without trying. I'm not sure if she was supposed to be the so-called leader of the group, but out of all of the girls, she stood out anyway, so I have no idea why she was playing herself. But even the most beautiful girls have self-esteem issues, and this business preys on them. I would watch her cling and be a part of as many conversations as she could. I'm not sure if she knew it, but she was the topic of many conversations—and not all good.

I was usually on the sideline, taking in everything. I really never got pulled into the conversations a lot. That was a good thing, because I realized quickly that you learn way more when you're doing all the listening instead of all the talking.

50 pulled me aside and was like, "Let me talk to you outside, Liv."

I got up and followed him outside. I really admired and looked up to Fif, so I took in anything he was about to tell me like a drug addict getting her fix.

"I know you're wondering why I bring you to these meetings or why Jimmy doesn't converse with you a lot, huh?"

"Well, yeah," I admitted. I mean, I knew Fif just wanted me to see how things went down, but I figured there might be more to it. But remember, I did more listening than talking, so I never really had to ask whatever was on my mind. If I watched and listened long enough, I'd get my answers. "I just fall back and let y'all do y'all's thang."

"Well, don't you worry about having to do all that. I will personally make sure all your shit is straight. I know you're a smart girl and you see the shit that is going on around here."

"Yeah, but I don't get it. I just want to get my project out and show people what I really got, but I think Jimmy is the one who just doesn't get it." Jimmy never asked me about my music or how I liked the label. I don't know if he didn't care or just didn't care what I did. Sometimes it made me feel invisible. I mean, any kind of interest or acknowledgment would have sufficed. It was way different for me. Jimmy Iovine was not giving me my daddy's only-girl treatment indeed.

I understood Jimmy was a busy man. He was manning an empire. I did appreciate, though, that Jimmy's VP, Ron Fair, came to my sessions to check on me and always showed interest. It just would have been nice to know that the owner of the label, who gave me my deal, cared about my stuff. I guess he was too busy caring about ol' girl's stuffing.

"Jimmy? Don't even worry about him," 50 said to me. "I oversee your project. Just tell me what you need and I got you. We gon' figure this out together. Okay?" He shot me his little everything-is-going-to-be-all-right smile.

"Okay, Fif. I hear you, 'cause I ain't about to be doing nothing that girl in there is doing." I nodded toward the inside, where I was sure by now ol' girl was sucking Jimmy off, literally and figuratively. "She should be ashamed of herself. Only thing I'm putting out is music! Now, if she really had feelings for ol' boy then maybe, just maybe I'd understand why she's putting herself out there like that, because trust me, I done seen how these females act when it comes to y'all men in the music industry," I harrumphed. "But you know as well as I do that with her, that ain't the case." I shook my head.

"Ah, you peeped that, huh?" Fif laughed.

"Oh, please. You know I done peeped quite a bit."

"You are as smart as I thought, and you're right. You will never be that broad."

Little did 50 know, I had long realized a lot of women in the entertainment industry did not have the same values and upbringing as I did. They were sleeping with A&R's, execs, and presidents of the company in order to get "a head"—literally!

What a shame. Here I was questioning what was wrong with me, and part of the problem was that some of these women were opening their legs in order to get deals done, tracks placed, records played, you name it. This bothered me so much, because I should had been getting judged on the quality of my music and my talents. Then I find out it's not even about that sometimes in this business. If that's what it took to keep a label interested, then perhaps I was supposed to be independent.

I can say, though, that a man can smell a chicken head before she even starts pecking, because no one ever tried that foolishness with me. See, a man knows when he can get away with taking advantage of someone. I was not the one, honey. Ain't nobody gon' use Olivia in no sexual way, period! Mama and Papa didn't raise no fool. Homie don't play dat (in my Damon Waynans "Homie D. Clown" voice). Nah, son, I wasn't with that in no kind of form or fashion.

Now, I am not trying to knock anyone's hustle. If that's how bad you want it, then that's on you. My belief in my talents were way too genuine to be doing what some of these industry girls were doing to get recognition.

If there is one thing that I learned from 50, it was to be assertive and always stand my ground. He always showed me better than he could tell me. There was one time in particular when we were doing an ad for Reebok.

"So, how do you want these ads to look, 50?" one of the Reebok female reps asked. We were in a meeting with Violator Management and Reebok, getting ready to roll out our ads for the women's and men's lines.

"Me and Olivia need to be front and center looking like money," 50 replied.

The rep started laughing. "Okay, we get it. But how do you want your ads to look? You know, positionwise: who, what, where?"

"I want Olivia in every ad with me, and I want Banks, Yayo, and Buck in the background in the men's line."

The female rep and the other two male reps looked at Fif and saw that he had a straight face and wasn't taking no for an answer. He wanted the ads with his entire crew, and that was that. He left no room for discussion. Everything about his stern tone and no-nonsense demeanor let them know that 50 was running the show. I imagined they'd been equipped to share all of their ideas, but again, nothing about 50's stance said that he was interested in what they wanted. This had the reps a little shook up.

Seeing the confused looks on their faces, 50 simply stood up from the table and said, "Y'all figure it out. You asked and I told you what I wanted, so just let me know when the photo shoot date is." He looked at me and said, "You ready? Let's go."

I had the straightest look on my face like, "Dayum-mmmm!"

As soon as we excited the office, 50 said over his shoulder to me, "Don't ever let anyone even try to tell you that you can't do something."

That was just one of the many times Fif schooled me. Another real moment we had was the time we were all hanging at the Los Angeles crib. 50 rented a crib in Malibu for us to use whenever we were in town. Fif and I found ourselves off having one of our many heart to hearts. 50's zodiac sign is cancer, so he can be very emotional, although he is the epitome of a gangster.

"You see this?" He showed me his hand. "This is where the bullet went in at."

I took his hand into mine and examined it.

"Can you see back there?" he asked, holding his mouth open wide.

I looked inside and saw the wound. As he was showing me his wounds and scars, I just paid attention closely. I held his hand and turned it over three or four times. "When it's cold, does your body hurt or tense up? I've heard people who have been shot before say that." I looked up at him. "Is it true?"

He nodded. "Yeah, the growing pains are still there from time to time, but you get used to it."

At this point, I was just looking at him in awe, thinking, *Oh my gosh. How could someone survive this and still overcome his "perception" in the industry?* He used his bad boy image to his advantage and turned the whole industry around to make them love him.

If he could do that, then imagine what I could do. There were people who thought I was finished because I'd had two record deals already and lost them both. To them it looked like things were just not going to work out for me, but I was determined to do two things: prove myself right and them bastards wrong!

I put my head back into the game. I pulled Paul back in as my manager and was doing a lot of touring still, so I wasn't stagnant on money. Everything was done independently since I was no longer signed. After a while I got frustrated with Paul not having the right connects or the drive to get me to the next level after all the success I had at the Unit. I ended up firing Paul in 2009, and as close as we were growing up, our relationship was never the same after that.

I pleaded with Paul for two years that he needed help and could not do it on his own at this point in my career. I was now internationally known because of all the exposure from being in G-Unit. Paul was very stubborn. It really killed me to fire him, because not only was Paul family, but he was one of my best friends. He was pissed, but I could not let my career drown because of his pride. I used to tell his oldest son PJ to try to talk some sense into him, but nothing worked.

Sometimes I wonder what goes through Paul's head since we haven't spoken. I am very close with PJ. We were always around one another as kids. He was my little cousin; how could I not? So now not talking to Paul but being in contact with his son has to make him feel some kind of way. I always ask PJ how his dad is doing, and I will continue to love him from a distance. It absolutely bothers me that Paul and I don't speak, but that wasn't my choice. Although I admit I am stubborn, Paul definitely got me beat in that category.

He had been there for me for everything in my life, both personal and business, but I had to stop letting him hold the family card over my head. As quiet as it's kept, if it wasn't for the fact that he was family, I would have fired him during my G-Unit run myself. I remember numerous times when I called Uncle Vern or Duane to vent about Paul. He had just gotten too comfortable.

I stayed touring off and on for a good two-year run overseas after being released from G-Unit. Sometimes it was a struggle financially, but that's why I kept the overseas dates flowing in. You make way more money overseas than in the states. I was definitely struggling in terms of finding the proper deal and being visible in the public eye. Out of sight, out of mind, right?

I know many people would say, "Why didn't you take the first deal offered?" Why would I wait so long? Who do I think I am? I am the shit! That's who I am. And I believe that every person striving after something should believe that in that area they are the shit! I told y'all before: Don't settle for less when God has made you for more.

My father always taught me never to settle. He said that I could have anything I wanted if I worked hard at it. Plus, I know for a fact God put me on this earth to make a mark. I had single deals thrown at me. That is where you sign to a label for them to work one single, and if it does well, they have an option to pick up an album deal. That wasn't cool with me, because I felt like if they didn't believe in the project enough to offer me an album deal from the jump, then it wasn't for me.

I've had album deals offered as well. To me the terms just didn't reflect my worth. A person should always know her worth going into a situation. Do not sit around and let someone put their own price tag on you. Well, I knew my worth and my capabilities, and I knew the type of music I was bringing to the table. I was not, am not, willing to settle! I would rather wait than be mad that I low-balled myself. I want to partner with a company who believes in me and my product one hundred percent.

Some people said that in the climate the music industry is in, I better take what I can get. I didn't have that mentality; never have and never will. My mentality is that God will always provide. None of the deals sat right with me in my spirit. A sure way of knowing whether you are making the right decision is if you have peace about it. If you walk away after signing on the dotted line with a belly ache, then nine times out of ten it wasn't the right thing to do. Every right decision, everything that lines up with what God has for you comes with some type of inner peace.

To me, signing onto another record deal would be my last shot. The third time had to be a charm. It had to be right. There were labels I wanted to be at: Atlantic, Universal Republic, Capitol. They would bite at my fishing rod, but in the end, they always let go. I told myself they weren't the right places or the right time, because if it was God, then the deal would have been pushed through. I am a serious woman of faith. It is tatted on my hand!

"Clive Davis and 50 Cent couldn't make her a star, so what can we do with her?" That was the word on the streets from some labels.

Everybody was a follower. Nobody wanted to stick their necks out. It's rare these days that an A&R dare speak up and say how he feels. People don't have balls anymore. I miss the days when people said, "I bet my job on this artist. She is a winner." They are so busy being yes men and kissing ass that they forget what the music is all about.

The truth is, I never got a fair shot at J Records, and I was dealt a bad hand at G-Unit. Now, I am not pointing the finger, but the issue was that we never had an R&B department at the Unit. 50 was the brains and everyone followed suit. If his marketing plan for himself was working so well, then they figured, why can't we use the same strategy on Olivia? It's bulletproof, right? Well, the problem was that Olivia wasn't a rapper, so that same formula wasn't as effective on a female R&B singer.

I was determined to let them and the rest of the world know who Olivia was. I knew I was going to have to work harder than I ever did before and really push myself. I was up for the challenge. God never gives us too much to bear. He gives us just enough until we learn the lesson that He was trying to teach us. Well, I am your humble servant, Lord. Faithful and willing to fall on my face trying, but I will always get back up.

I try to find the lesson in every mistake, every win, and every loss. That's some of the very things that mold us into the people we are. That's what makes some of us the survivors that we are today. There are so many things that people can bounce back from. People will be quick to tell you that your career is over. That cancer has taken over your body and you only have a few months to live. That since you were fired from your job you are never going to be able to make ends meet. That the love of your life has cheated on you and shattered your world in a split second. There are so many obstacles that we all are faced with, but no one has the power to tell you when it's done. If God didn't tell you it's done, then you have plenty of time left. If you are alive and well, then there is still work to be done.

Well, God hasn't told me it's done, and I am absolutely alive and well, so I guess that can only mean one thing: I'm just getting started!

Chapter 13

I focused one hundred percent on music. Along with my record deals went my management as well, so I was now in the middle of looking for new management. No matter how focused I tried to remain, however, cupid has a way of shooting that damn arrow and hitting folks right in the ass!

Over the years, Shaggy and I had had our on-and-off-again, just-kicking-it thing going on. Because of all the back and forth, the making up and the breaking up, I knew it wouldn't last forever. Our forever was about three years long, though, which seemed like an eternity with all I went through.

I understood when Shaggy and I first started messing around that there was no commitment involved, but once we agreed that we were going to be exclusive, that meant we were supposed to cut everybody else off. I had no problem doing so because I didn't have commitment issues. Shaggy, on the other hand, was a completely different story.

"Look, Shaggy, I'm not trying to sit here while some other broad is still thinking you are her man," I fussed while he packed his bags. He was headed to Jamaica because he said there were some loose ends he needed to tie up. Well, there was one in particular I needed him to make a priority in handling. Forget about tying it up; he needed to put a knot in this one, then tie a brick around it and drop it in the bottom of the ocean Sopranos style!

This woman was his girl back home. I thought he was done with her, but his boy Robbie had slipped and told me he was still seeing her.

"I don't care how long you and ol' girl kicked it over there in Jamaica. You need to cut her off—completely." I did the knife motion across the throat with my index finger.

"I told you I'd take care of it," Shaggy said. "I'm going to tell her how it is, just not over the phone. I'll see her when I get to Jamaica and I'll make it clear to her that it's over." He walked over to me. I was sitting on his bed, not the happiest camper in the tent. "You're my baby. Only you." He kissed me on the forehead to try to reassure me he would take care of things.

I looked him in his eyes. "You promise?"

"Promise," he said, and then an hour later he was off to the airport.

I was worrying like crazy before the plane even took off. I knew I was in a bad situation with him. I knew in my gut that he would never leave either of us. I would have to completely cut him off myself. That wouldn't be easy, though, because he was something and someone I was used to.

Whenever Shaggy and I were in town at the same time, I was basically sleeping at his house every night. If I didn't show up, he would call and ask me if I was coming home. Yes, *home* was his house. I didn't want for anything when we were together. He took care of any and everything for me. The only thing that he wasn't taking care of properly was my heart, but I just kept holding on, hoping things would change, hoping that one day his word would mean something.

I thought the feeling was mutual, that I was his ace. After all, he never acted funny or suspicious when it came to me. He told me he loved me constantly and was always affectionate. He never hid me or acted shady or paranoid when we were in public, so why wouldn't I think I was the only chick in his life? And I never would have thought otherwise if it hadn't been for his boy, Robbie.

Robbie and I were super close, so much so that at one point, Shaggy even asked me if Robbie and I had ever slept together.

"You ever give Robbie mi tings?" Shaggy asked, extra serious one night in bed.

I turned my head so quick to face him that I thought my neck was going to snap off. "Negro, have you been drinking again? Why the hell would you ask me a dumb-ass question like that? He's your best friend, you idiot. That's just nasty! Plus, don't nobody want no damn Robbie." I was annoyed that he even asked me that foolishness. Had Robbie tried to push up on one of his girls in the past? Even if he had, why the hell would he think I would do him dirty like that?

"Mi just a mek sure. I nuh like nuh bwoy too close wid my woman."

The ones who ask questions like that are usually the ones actually doing the cheating, scared the other person is out doing the same kind of dirt they are. This was all confirmed the day I was hanging out with Robbie while Shaggy was in Jamaica, supposedly breaking things off with that chick. Robbie slipped up and told me Shaggy was still seeing her. It wasn't a conversation; he just said it so nonchalant, like I knew what was going on. I kept my composure so Robbie was none the wiser.

Inside I was furious! I didn't even call Shaggy and spazz on him. I just got my facts together and waited for him to get off that plane and bring his ass back home.

"So what happened? Did you break it off with her?" We hadn't even been in his house five minutes. Nope, luggage wasn't even unpacked.

"Look, Liv, it wasn't the right time to do it."

"Well, what the hell is that supposed to mean?" I fumed. "It's never going to be a right time to break up with anybody, you dummy."

"Just let it go. I said I am going to do it. It just wasn't right." I felt like one of them dumb broads from some reality TV show. I'm not trying to be funny. I was them once upon a time, but at least I can blame it on age . . . and some stupidity.

Shaggy had played me one too many times, but more importantly, I had played my damn self. It was time to go back to the roots that my parents had instilled in me—all that confidence and high self-esteem. I needed me a refill fo' sho!

There weren't even any words to say to Shaggy at that point. I cut my eyes at him and stormed out of his place. I had vowed in my heart, my mind, my body, and my soul that it was over between us for good. I really meant it this time . . . just like the last. Ugh! I did not want there to be a next time, but . . .

I don't know what it was about Shaggy that always drew me back, but I knew that at some point I was going to have to shake him off, because I couldn't continue to do this to myself. I could have any man I wanted. Hell, I'd had men lined up after shows promising me the world, yet I wanted his cheating ass. I always told him and myself that I could change him, but did he really want to change? Perhaps I should have been asking myself that question, because I went back to him a million times more, only to get more of the same.

Another night, after getting back together for the umpteenth time, Shaggy and I had just finished having movie night at his crib with our crew. We showed everyone out and headed upstairs to cozy up to one another.

"I'm going to take a shower, babe, so you get ready for Mr. Lova Lova," he said.

"Oh my God, you are so corny." I teased, though I liked when he said silly stuff like that.

Now, I have never—let me repeat, *never*—gone through a man's phone. No man I'd been with had ever given me reason to, but on this particular night, something was telling me to. As Shaggy went into the bathroom, his Blackberry on the nightstand was just calling me. Shaggy never put a lock on his phone because he was always forgetting and locking himself out, but after this incident, I'm sure he does now.

The minute I heard the water start running, I grabbed his phone and began to scroll through his text messages. What I found nearly made me want to get a knife from downstairs and go into that bathroom and spazz the hell out.

There was a message from some college girl asking him to bring condoms the next time he came to her dorm because they were out. So, not only was he still messing with his old lady back on the island, but his dirty old ass had a college chick too.

That was the last straw for me. My heart was hammering. My blood pressure was through the roof. Before I did anything I would surely regret, I had to get out of there. I could see the headlines right now: r&b sensation olivia longott stabs her boyfriend, reggae superstar shaggy, for his dirty dog ways. Then I'd get ten years in prison. No way. "Not I," said the cat! I was twenty-five years old with way too much life ahead of me to ruin it, but believe me when I say I understand now how a person can snap. I visualized the damage I could do to that man, then I got my ass out of the bed and was gone. Did we really need to have that conversation again? Like Maya Angelou said, "When a person shows you who they are, believe them." Well, damn it, I was finally a true believer! Shaggy broke my heart in the worst way. As I ran out of the house, I could not control the tears falling down my face. I felt so lost and so alone, and there I stood outside of his house with nowhere to go and nowhere to turn. Shaggy had picked me up that night, so my car was at my place. I called my cousin Jackie at three o'clock in the morning.

"Livy? What's wrong?" she asked when she picked up the phone.

I was crying hysterically. I couldn't even get my words out. I was just boo-hooing into the receiver.

"Olivia, you're scaring me. Please tell me what's going on."

"Jackie, come pick me up. I need you to come pick me up now."

My poor cousin was dead in her sleep, and I'm sure she didn't know what the hell was going on.

"I'm by Shaggy's, standing outside waiting on you to come get me. Please hurry," I said then hung up the phone. There was no use trying to talk to her on the phone. I could hardly breathe, let alone talk.

Thank God she didn't live far away. I figured it would take her less than ten minutes to get there. I stood outside with tears falling down my face, praying he wouldn't catch me outside and try to stop me before she got there.

Jackie scooped me up and then headed toward my place. During the drive back, Shaggy was blowing my phone up, but I kept sending him straight to voice mail. Ten minutes after Jackie dropped me off at my place, the doorbell started ringing. I ignored it at first, but then there was knocking on the door.

"Shaggy, go away!" I yelled.

"Liv, it's me, Jackie," I heard her call through the door.

"Thank God," I said as I flung open the door to find Jackie standing there with this deep look of concern on her face.

"I couldn't just leave you here like this, cuz. Talk to me. Tell me everything."

I couldn't even talk. I just went in for a hug and stood there and cried on her shoulders. "Can we go for a ride or something?" I said, pulling out of the hug and wiping my nose. "I gotta get out of here." I wanted to be gone just in case Shaggy decided to come over.

"Sure, come on," Jackie said.

I grabbed my purse and keys. We went to her house, where I just cried and whined to Jackie all night. I had vowed that I would never be in this position again. Shaggy and I were finished, and there was nothing he could say or do to get me back. At least that's what I'd convinced myself of that night anyway.

But some things are much easier said than done.

Chapter 14

It took me months to start talking to Shaggy again. Yes, I said *again*, but this time it was just as friends. I was trying to salvage what little trust in him I had left. There was nothing sexual. I was just hanging around him and his friends like back in the beginning, when shit was great. You would think I was a glutton for punishment, but I did love him and wanted us to at least be friends. He'd apologized over and over; calling me, texting me, even emailing me. Even though I'd made the personal vow to wipe him out of my life completely, slowly but surely I was drawn in again.

Everything was everything at first, but then there was this couple of days when Shaggy was just acting too weird. He always had this expression on his face like he'd eaten a rotten apple. When he talked to me, I noticed he kept it short and could barely look in my eyes. I got tired of trying to figure out what was going on, so I just called him on it.

"What's really going on?" I asked. We were at his place. "You've been acting funny lately. I can tell something's wrong. You can talk to me. What's up?" Here I was being all concerned, totally unprepared for what he was about to hit me with.

"She's pregnant," Shaggy said under his breath.

"Excuse me?" No way had I heard what I thought I'd heard.

"She, uh, called me last night, and uh . . . you know. She just told me she was pregnant.

It was very simple to do that math. How far she was in her pregnancy lined up with the last time he'd gone to Jamaica. "Oh, so is that why you couldn't break it off with her in Jamaica? Because you were too busy giving her your seed?" Believe it or not, I was not loud or snapping off this time. I think I was all snapped out. I was so calm it was almost scary.

He'd never seen me so relaxed. He just sat there with this stupid look on his face, and with that same stupid look, he watched my ass walk away for good. Just like that, I was gone. I was numb, but gone, and I wasn't playing around this time.

I cut off all communication with him. I didn't even want to be his friend. It had taken far more convincing than necessary, but I was finally convinced. That fool wasn't going to change, and every bone in my body had finally accepted it. When I say I have never spoken a single word to that man since, I'm not exaggerating. Now, I did still continue to speak to a couple of his friends that had become my friends through him, especially Robbie. I even still went by the house to use the studio when he wasn't there. If he was in town, I made sure I stayed far away.

Don't even get it twisted. I didn't do any drive-bys or drop-bys in hopes of running into Shaggy. If he was in town, I made sure I was ghost. After all the hell he put me through, Shaggy and I couldn't be friends. I was completely done. I wanted him to feel what it felt like to completely lose me for good.

His boys, Rossie and Robbie, called me almost daily to tell me how I'd broken Shaggy's heart, and that he loved and missed me tremendously.

"I've never seen him so depressed," Rossie told me.

"Well, there is a first time for everything, and honestly I don't give a fuck."

I'd definitely cried enough tears over him. I can't say that I know if he was actually crying over me. Robbie and Rossie would have never told me that, because Jamaican men always liked to say, "Bad man no cry."

I knew Shaggy must have been going through it, though, for them to keep hounding me like they were. I couldn't have cared less. I was colder than ice at that point. As Banks would say, "I'm cooler than the other side of the pillow."

I got so fed up with them calling me to tell me how hurt he was that I eventually blew up.

"He hurts? Well, what do you think he did to me? He cheated on me numerous times and now his ol' lady is pregnant with his baby. And I'm the one who broke his heart?" I couldn't believe they even thought for one minute I was supposed to feel bad about leaving him. "Don't ever come to me with this bullshit again." At that point, even though we had managed to stay pretty cool, I never wanted to hear from Shaggy's friends again!

Good riddance. His baby mama could have him. She could have as many babies as she wanted, trying to keep him. He was never going to marry her anyway. He'd told me that himself.

And guess what? To this day he still hasn't married her. But no shade, though. LOL.

Robbie and Rossie would still call me once in a blue moon. I actually had to stop talking to Robbie because he told Shaggy private things that he and I had discussed. Call me stupid, but I felt his alliance should have been with me. I mean, he was best friends with both of us, so I trusted that what I told him stayed with us, as whatever shaggy told him stayed with them. He never purposely came reporting Shaggy's business back to me, so I expected the same regarding my business.

See, I am no saint. I did my share of dirt when we were together. The difference is I never got caught. And yes, I only cheated because he cheated. I did not even regret it. I just wanted to get even. Hey, when you are young . . . It was never about being the mature person. It was about who was going to get who back, and I felt that if I did the same thing he had, then it wouldn't hurt so much. But it still hurt.

Two wrongs don't make a right, but still, why should I be faithful knowing he was still messing around? This was one of the reasons I stopped talking to Robbie. I slipped up and got too comfortable and cocky around him and shared who I was seeing, and his snitch ass went and told Shaggy. Ain't that something?

"Now, all this shit your boy done did to me, and that's how you do me, fam?" I said to Robbie, yet again feeling betrayed. In the infamous lyrics of Jay-Z. "I was gon' get right back, but you don't get a nigga back like that."

I know Robbie was Shaggy's friend first and I'd met him through Shaggy, but at one point Robbie and I were closer than he and Shaggy were. The two of them even had a huge falling out and didn't speak for a few years. Who was still there for Robbie? Me, that's who! (In my Al Pacino voice). Robbie and I told each other a lot of things.

Back then, Robbie would tell me about all the different ladies he was seeing. He was quite the ladies' man. He had only introduced me to Jade once back in the day, and it was a quick "Hey, Livy, this is my friend Jade." I didn't know her at all, so we really weren't friends to say the least. Robbie was my friend, and that was who my loyalty was to. So how would he have felt if I went and spilled everything he had been doing behind her back to her? Even though it was years later that Jade and I would become friends, I could have still ratted on him. I was too loyal, even if he wasn't.

Robbie's and my relationship became strained. I would never be able to trust him again, and so just like with Shaggy, my mind was made up about him as well.

Robbie's child's mother, Jade, and I became good friends, even though I wasn't that close to her man anymore. I had borne witness to Robbie playing that girl when we weren't friends, and I never said a word to her, because I didn't know her back then. I was definitely a better friend to Robbie than he was to me.

Jade knew Robbie had horrible ways. Shaggy and Robbie were basically twins in that way. When we became best friends, we swapped a few stories about Robbie, but she never wanted to know the things in the past he'd told me he did to her. Jade was the most forgiving person, and I admired her for that. I know for sure I could have never been so forgiving if I had actually gotten pregnant by Shaggy and had his kid and he still did me dirty. No, suh. God bless her! I really do love the way she holds it together and lets Robbie come see and take his son whenever he wants. Jade has such a huge heart and is a beautiful person inside and out. I just love my "wittle bestie." Yeah I said that in my "baby talk" voice. Don't act like y'all don't be doing that same voice.

Eventually Jade got sick of Robbie's games and those two ended up being on the outs. When they broke up, that fool had the nerve to tell Jade that she stole me from him; that I was his friend. Really now? Just priceless. He was just like Shaggy. When will they ever grow up?

I will never understand how Shaggy made me feel like the happiest person in the world and in that same moment he could break my heart . . . and I still continued to love him with all the little pieces left. There would be this tiny part of me that would always love Shaggy because of our history together, but I was finally free, a burden off of my heart and my shoulders. I knew I deserved better.

In hindsight, yeah, Shaggy might have loved me. I mean, he wasn't all bad. He wasn't this terrible guy, and when things were great, they were really great. I think what he loved most was the fact that my spirit and presence made him feel young again—not to mention the fact that his closest friends loved me. Shaggy was a homebody, but I made him go out more and enjoy this wonderful life God had blessed us with.

It doesn't matter how beautiful you are. Shit, sometimes that's the last thing they look at. If a man wants to cheat, he is going to do it regardless if he loves you or not. I used to think I just wasn't enough for him, but in the end I realized no one would ever be enough for Shaggy. That is just who he is. When I realized that, I was able to let it go and heal. So once again, I found myself putting all these emotions into my music and trying to move forward.

Chapter 15

I do not know what it means to give up. I will always keep pushing until I get what I want, whether it's in my love life, career, or anything. My father always told me I could do or be anything I wanted. I believed him, and have always carried myself in such a way. Some people have mistaken my acting out this belief for cockiness. I've heard many people say, "Oh, who does she think she is? She is too sure of herself. Chick think she's Beyoncé." Uh, no, damn it! I am Olivia and unapologetic!

Well, excuse me for having high self-esteem, positive thinking, and for loving myself. I love me, damn it! The world we live in today is so messed up. Everybody always has to say something bad about someone else in order to make them feel better about themselves. Well, newsflash: I don't have that problem. I am proud to be a confident young woman, but it's almost like some people would rather see me broken in order to understand or to be able to relate to my struggle.

I can't apologize for not being one of those people who allows the struggles of life to get to me. No matter what I'm going through, I can turn on the news and see someone going through something a hundred times worse. People are losing loved ones, their homes. Women are losing their lives from domestic abuse, their kids to diseases, their battles with cancer. Natural disasters and fire blazes . . . come on! When you look at your own life and then witness those types of situations and circumstance, who am I to dare have a pitiful "woe is me" party?

I thank God for my self-assurance and assertiveness. When other young girls and women look to me, I want them to say, "That Olivia always pressed through." I absolutely don't want anybody looking to me as the person who was always whining and complaining about life. I honestly couldn't care less what strangers think of me. I know me, and my family knows me, and that's all that matters. Life is way too precious, and I refuse to grieve God by complaining about the life He gave me—the life He chose to bless me with.

God knew what He was doing when He built me this way. God built me to last, honey. You have to be harder than the Man of Steel himself in this music industry. If not, bitterness and regret can and will eat you alive.

It was truly frustrating trying to get myself out of the whole G-Unit brand once I was no longer part of it, but once I finally did it, it felt great. Knowing I was standing on my own two feet again and that the public loved me as Olivia the solo artist was like a breath of fresh air. Not only that, but it felt good knowing that there were people in the industry who I could still call up and talk to. David Lawrence, who worked at Atlantic Records at the time, was one of them. I was always calling on him to ask business questions to help propel me into my solo career.

"Wassup, D.L.?" I sounded all hardcore through the phone. D.L was my homie.

"Hey, Liv. What do I owe the pleasure of this call today?" he said in his sarcastic tone.

"Oh, you know me so well, D. Always calling to pick your brain. And since you asked, I am looking for a new manager, and I think you can help me weed the meatballs out," I said.

"Hmmm, give me a few days. I already got some people that just came to mind. I'm going to make a few calls and get back to you, cool?"

"Okay, D. I'm counting on you. No meatballs."

"Liv, this is ya boy here. You know I got this," he said before we ended the call.

Within a week, as promised, David called me back.

"Sis, I got him," David said, sounding all sure of himself. I've got the perfect manager for you."

"Now, I don't even wanna mess with anymore of those larger management companies, so I hope that's not what you bringing to me," I said. "I need somebody in the game who knows what they are doing and has the time to focus on me and my career, not a whole other slew of folks."

"Sis, I'm telling you I got you. This cat is the one."

He sounded more confident than ever. Had me all geeked up. "Aw, shit," I said. "You found him, son?"

"Yup. His name is Richard, but he goes by the name of Rich Dollaz. He used to work at Bad Boy, and he really knows radio." He paused for a minute. "I think this could work."

"All right," I said. "I trust your opinion. Hook up the meeting."

A week later, I met Rich at Mimi's one of my favorite spots in Manhattan. I had Duane accompany me. We spoke for a good two hours on Rich's background and where I wanted to go next with my career. I liked his spunk and passion. I thought about it for a good week then came to the conclusion that David was right; Rich was the perfect fit for me at this moment in time and what I hoped to accomplish in my career. Two months later, I signed a management agreement with him.

First on the agenda was locking in at the studio so I could create more records for my album. I already had a couple records that I wanted to use, but I needed a full album. Rich couldn't go see these labels if I didn't have new music. When it came to picking and choosing songs, Rich and I fought like brother and sister.

"Oh my God, you are bugging," I told him. "My Janet-esque record, 'Alone with U,' is my joint. That's staying."

"Nah, we gotta put 'Say My Name' on here." Rich tried to belt it out and did a horrible job. He was not convincing at all.

"You are killing me, Richard," I said.

We did this regularly. Another sure thing I knew I could count on with Rich, though, was not just to argue with me about songs, but to argue with me about who I was dating. Man, this dude was worse than a father. My dad never asked about my love life. If I brought someone home to meet him, he knew what that was. Richard didn't think anybody was good enough to date his li'l Livy. No, sir. I loved the fact that he held me in high standards, though. He would be like, "I want you to be with Kobe Bryant or A-Rod."

"Rich, you do know that Kobe is married and A-Rod is in a relationship." I side-eyed him.

"Well, that's the grade of dude you should be with. I hold you in that regard," he said, standing his ground.

"I would think you would want me to be with someone who loved and took care of me, not because of their status. What about that?" I challenged him right back.

He got frustrated and was like, "Damn it, li'l girl, don't give me no lip. Just get focused, man."

We both busted out laughing so hard. Rich is a piece of work, man!

I decided I had to start hiding my dates from Rich and not let him know who I was kicking it with, just so I wouldn't have to hear his mouth. Besides, he never let me in on his secret rendezvous, so why did he have to be all up in mine? Sheesh, can I live?

Rich never dated anyone for long. The longest I ever saw him with someone was two weeks, and then he was on to the next. Rich doesn't like stability with women in that sense. He loves all women, so I couldn't keep track even if I tried. There was one girl I really liked for Rich. They have been friends since college. Jessie is such a sweet, simple, intelligent, pretty girl. He keeps her around for some reason. She is there for him when he needs her the most. That's the girl he should be with and he knows it. I hope he realizes it one day before it's too late, but for right now, Rich gon' stick with the fast girls.

Chapter 16

It was during the summer of 2011—July 22, to be exact—and I'd had one of the worst weeks ever. On top of that, Rich and I had just found out that Butch Lewis, his mentor, father figure, and support system, had just passed away. Thank God he went peacefully in his sleep, but no one is ever prepared for that kind of news.

Rich was not taking it well, but we still had obligations that needed to be met. We had an event booked in Tampa that week, and Rich and I agreed that we would do the event and fly back first thing in the morning. For the entire plane ride we talked about how crazy this was because we had just spoken to Butch the day before; then Rich got a call in the wee hours of the morning that he'd passed away in his sleep. It felt like the longest flight ever.

We finally arrived at our hotel in Tampa and just wanted to go to our rooms and rest until my event that night. The event was for Tarence Kinsey, an NBA player in Tampa. I normally got booked to host celebrity events, but there were always a lot of basketball player events. I guess they knew I loved sports. Heck, I played basketball up until college. I was the three-point champ in junior high school. Sheesh, it ain't my fault they are always booking me for something! Mix my two favorite loves, music and sports, and it was the threesome of a lifetime for me.

I had never met Tarence before, he previously played for the Memphis Grizzlies and Cleveland Cavaliers. His assistant, Tabitha, was pleasant and very professional.

Tabitha greeted us in the hotel lobby when we arrived, and told us what to expect for the night. She gave us our keys, and we each went straight to our rooms to sleep. I was so exhausted that I didn't wake up until about forty-five minutes before it was time for us to meet Tarence's people downstairs in the lobby. As a matter of fact, it was his people calling my room that woke me up.

"Hello," I answered in a groggy voice.

"I'm sorry. Did I wake you?" she said

"It's okay. I should be getting up now anyway," I replied.

"Well, my name is Carlisia, and I was just calling to let you know that Mr. Kinsey wanted to greet you himself, so he'll be meeting with you to thank you personally for coming before he heads over to the party."

I perked up a little and tried to clear the frog out of my throat. "Okay, cool. That's fine." I looked over at the clock, the first sign that I had to get to moving quick, fast, and in a hurry.

"Then we'll see you in a bit. He'll be up to your room in about twenty minutes."

Wiping the sleep out of my eyes, I said, "No problem," although clearly it was a problem.

I ended the call and jumped straight out of the bed to start getting ready. I figured I had a few extra minutes, because with most of the men I'd dealt with in the past, their twenty minutes was more like forty. What I didn't know about Tarence is that for him, twenty minutes means twenty minutes.

It was twenty minutes on the nose when I heard a knock at the door.

"Damn, that better be Rich," I mumbled as I stood in the bathroom mirror putting on my Show Orchid MAC lipstick. I prayed that it was housekeeping or something. Anybody but Tarence, because I needed fifteen more minutes to get my hair right.

I was halfway to the door when I noticed the clock again. Time was a-ticking. Realizing I was down to the wire when it came to time, I didn't care if it was Rich or housekeeping. I didn't have time to stop and talk to either one of them, so I yelled out, "Give me fifteen minutes."

"No problem. Take your time." It was a male voice, and it didn't belong to Rich. Something told me it wasn't housekeeping either.

OMG! Had I just told the guest of honor, who was making a special trip to give me a face to face, to wait on me? Lord, that boy was going to think I was some kind of diva.

What was done was done, though, and I sure wasn't about to let him in to see me with my hair pinned up, looking all crazy. You know what they say about first impressions. I went back into the bathroom and finished primping, not realizing that I had exceeded the fifteen minutes.

"All right, come on now." There was another country accent. I know he was probably a bit antsy by now, but all I thought to myself was how cute his accent sounded coming from the other side of that door.

I just happened to be finished and coming out of the bathroom anyway. As I headed to the door, I could hear him throw out one last country-accented "Dang!"

I had to hold my mouth from laughing out loud. No I hadn't kept that man waiting almost twenty minutes. We had to be over at the venue in five! I ran my hands down my clothes, making sure everything was on point.

I had on a sheer multicolored Nieves Lavi flowing gown from their resort collection. I wore a gray leather belt to show off my twenty-six-inch waist, and gray Camilla Skovgaard leather heels.

I opened the door and smiled at him. "I'm ready now."

It was him and a woman who introduced herself as Carlisia, the same woman who had called me earlier. She was sweet and told me I looked beautiful. I noticed they were both wearing white, but I thought nothing of it. I also noticed his suit was perfectly tailored. White pants and jacket, white button-up shirt with three buttons opened at the top: He was giving me swagged-out *Miami Vice* 2011. The brown silk pocket scarf and thin brown belt accompanied with brown shoes made him as sharp as a tack.

He looked at me with the warmest smile and simply said, "Well, hello." Actually, he said something else too. It was the most tear-jerking thing I had heard in a long time, but I promised him I'd never tell a soul. I wouldn't want his homies trying to take away his man card, but his boy Jamal already knows what it was. I'm blushing just thinking about it.

We all walked to the elevator and met Rich downstairs in the lobby. Rich had on a checkered button-down shirt with beige khakis. When Tarence's boys gathered in the lobby, I noticed they all had on white too. That's when a light bulb went off in my head.

"Hold up. Did we miss the all-white memo?" I asked.

Tarence looked both Rich and me up and down. "Yes, ma'am," he replied. "I figured you just wanted to be different since you are the artist. You know, stand out."

I felt so crazy-looking. "Oh, wow. No one gave us the memo. I am so sorry. I feel like I need to go back and change."

"Naw, don't worry about it. Like my sister said, you look beautiful."

After I finished blushing from his compliment, Rich, Tarence, and I rode over to the event together. At the time I was thinking, *Awww, he's a pretty nice guy*, but I was definitely not thinking about a love connection. I had to stay focused, host this event, and still manage to cheer Rich up. Tarence seemed so pleasant. He was handsome and a gentleman, but like I said, I wasn't there to make a love connection. I was there to do a job, so I just smiled and remained cordial.

Of course, with the situation being what it was, Rich was clearly not in a good mood. He just wanted to go back to the room and be alone. That was exactly what I was not going to let him do. So, while we were in the VIP section of this huge hall, sitting at our table on the couches, I passed him the liquor, and with my glass in the air I said, "Cheer up. People want to see you smiling."

He broke off some little halfhearted corny smile.

"You look like you don't want to be here. I don't even want to leave you sitting here alone," I told him.

"Look, you here to do a job. Go handle your business," Rich told me.

Reluctantly I stood up and began to make my rounds around the room. Rich was right. Tarence had brought me there to help host the party, and so I had to do my job. A few minutes later, I ended up at the bar with Tarence.

On the drive to the event, I had told Tarence that I needed a shot because I had had a stressful couple of days dealing with Butch's untimely passing. He recalled that conversation and said, "So, what about those shots? What are we drinking?"

"Patrón, please," I said.

He sized me up then told the waitress, "Four shots of Patrón, please."

Oh, Lord. What did I get myself into? I thought as I watched the waitress make the drinks.

The waitress set two shots each in front of Tarence and me.

"Here's to a great event," I said before raising my glass and tossing back my first shot.

After we finished our shots, we went back over to VIP and joined Rich. Tarence's mom and Tabitha found their way over to the table, and they joined in on the conversation. After a few minutes, Tarence got pulled away for some photo ops.

Tabitha and I were making small talk when Tarence's mom stood in front of me and just came right out of left field with her own topic of conversation.

"Oh, you don't know it yet, but I prayed about you," Tarence's mom said to me.

I just nodded, having no idea where this conversation was going.

"You and my son are going to be something special."

Then in jumps Tabitha. "What is your favorite color? Because mine is yellow, so I think that would make a great bridesmaid's gown."

I'm looking over at Rich with the same confused look on my face as he had on his. Had I had one shot too many? Was I really listening to them plan our wedding right in front of me like it was nothing? What I would find out later is that his mom is usually on point with her visions and prayers. Anyway, I hadn't even held that man's hand yet. All we'd done was take shots together. I decided from that point on I had to watch my drinks. Maybe shorty at the bar made my shots a little stronger than I thought.

Chapter 17

At one point, when all eyes were on me, I had to join in the conversation with Tarence's mom and Tabitha, so I threw in that my favorite color was green. If you can't beat 'em, join 'em, right? LOL!

"Oh, yes, green," his mom said. "That's a nice color too. There are lots of lovely shades of green." She went on to tell me that God had let her know I was going to be her son's wife. "It's going to be you and Tarence. Oh, I know what I'm talking about. So, that is that."

Rich let out a, "Aye, yo," then whispered to me, "Is this really happening? What the hell kind of party did we agree to do?"

I just shrugged my shoulders and smiled and let Tarence's mom and Tabitha finish the conversation. As farfetched as it may have been, I was actually flattered. What woman didn't want a handsome man's mother saying, "You are going to be my son's wife." Granted it could have been taken a whole other way, but his mom had such a sweet spirit and wonderful aura about her. I knew she wasn't some crazy lady. Besides, his mom was a young, cool mother. I could tell. She had on all white as well: a white fitted tank with white jeans and a brown thin Gucci belt. She donned a fly li'l bob type of hairstyle too. In my head I was like, *Go 'head, moms, wit' yo' bad self.*

Tarence's mom continued going on and on about this wedding that God had shown her was going to take place between her son and me. I looked over across the room and noticed Tarence glimpsing over at me.

"Excuse me, guys. I think Tarence is looking for me."
I had to say something to get away from there, because
I had absolutely no response for the conversation at
hand. I got up from the couch and made my way over to
Tarence. He must have seen the stunned look on my face.

"You all right?" Tarence asked me. "I hope my family
wasn't driving you nuts with questions."

I just smiled and said, "They are something else. They
sure say what they feel."

He didn't even bother to ask what I meant. He just
looked over at them and shook his head.

A few minutes later Tarence and I made our way to
the DJ booth. The crowd was really enjoying themselves.
Everyone was doing this dance called The Wobble. It was
pretty much the 2011 Electric Slide. His grandma, Betty
Kinsey, was on the dance floor cutting a rug, honey! She
was giving them young girls out there a run for their
money. I mean, she was twirling and getting down to
the ground literally. I was watching her so I could try the
dance out myself later.

At some point, I laughed so hard watching her that I
leaned over and put my head on Tarence's chest. Later,
Tarence would tell me how that was one of his favorite
moments of the night. We did have a great time at his
party, so we decided to keep it going.

It was about three o'clock in the morning when the
party shut down, so we headed to the Hard Rock Casino
to get some food. We walked in about ten deep. Rich had
started to warm up to everybody by now, so Mr. Feeling
Good decided he wanted to gamble.

"I'm feeling lucky," Rich said, rubbing his hands
together.

We stopped at the first blackjack table we came upon.
As quickly as Rich put that two hundred dollars on the
table is just how quickly he lost it! Everybody laughed at
him.

"Not so lucky after all, huh, Rich?" Tarence joked and gave him a "Better luck next time," and a dap.

"Shit happens." Rich shrugged. "I was bound to spend it on something useless anyway."

Nobody was trying to gamble after that, so we all headed to the restaurant. It was after four in the morning when we left. Tarence and Rich and I got back in the awaiting SUV and headed for the hotel. Rich and I said good-bye to everyone in the lobby then went ahead to our rooms to call it a night.

No sooner than I had entered my room, my phone started vibrating, alerting me that I had an incoming text. I pulled out my phone and read it.

> this is tarence. if you're not too tired i was wondering if i could come up just to talk.

His assistant more than likely had given him my phone number because I sure hadn't, and I knew Rich wouldn't have given it out without asking me first. As I read the last line of the text I just started smiling and shaking my head. He must have re-read it himself and knew what I was going to be thinking. As the laugh exited my mouth, another text from him came through.

> okay maybe not just to talk. that sounded like a cliché lol. just to hang. we can even hang in the lobby if you want to.

He was a man who knew how to quickly clean up a mess. I liked that in him already. With a blushing smile on my face, I replied to his text.

> sure. but i need to change into some sweats first. give me 15 and you can come up.

Okay, so maybe I was feeling a little flustered. There was something intriguing about that man. As I went to change my clothes, my phone vibrated one more time. It was Tarence again, of course.

good. see you in 15.

I hit him back with a smiley face and went to change clothes. Now, I should have known from earlier that his ass was prompt, because fifteen minutes later there was a knock at my door.

"Hi again," I said, opening the door and letting him in.

"I never wanted to say good-bye in the first place," he said, walking over and sitting down on the couch, while I sat on the bed.

"Your grandmother is something else," I said. "Oh my gosh. I could party with her any day."

"Man, that's nothing. She is like that all the time." I just loved hearing Tarence talk. His country accent and deep voice was so attractive to me.

"She reminds me of my grandmother with all her spunk. Dang, I miss her." I stared off. It had been a while since I'd seen my grandmother. Bringing her up brought back memories.

"Where is your grandma?" he asked.

"Oh, she's in Jamaica. That's where my family is from."

We got into a whole conversation about Jamaica and how the lizards used to scare me and be on my ceiling at night. Then I talked about how I hated snakes and feel like they are the devil. He in turn told me he didn't like snakes either, but his fear was alligators. We ended up talking about a million and one things. Our conversation was so all over the place, but so right. We were getting to know one another. We were so into each other that before we knew it, the sun was coming up.

We stayed up talking until seven that morning. It was the perfect ending to a night that I didn't think we'd even enjoy due to dealing with the loss of Butch.

I walked him to the door and he turned around and leaned in for a kiss. I sure didn't hesitate. With his fine ass. I had to use that line. He always says it to me. I still love that he sends me texts that read "fine ass."

"You think maybe you'll have time to do lunch before your flight heads out tomorrow?" he asked me.

I said, "Yes," without delay. "You wanna scoop me at around eleven thirty?"

"I wish I could just scoop you up now." He smiled. "But good things come to those who wait," he said, and then we called it a night—or should I say morning.

I laid my head down for a few hours, waking back up at around eleven in order to get ready real quick.

Just like clockwork, he hit me with a text at precisely 11:30, letting me know he was waiting for me downstairs. I told him that I was almost ready, and that he could come in and wait in the lobby.

When I got downstairs, he was waiting for me in the lobby. We went outside and had to wait for the valet to bring his car back around.

"Is it always this hot out here?" I asked as we waited for his car. "It's gotta be like ninety-five degrees out here." I had on a pair of checkered, fitted Capri pants, a pink ribbed tank, and nude pumps. But hell, I needed a two-piece bathing suit to endure this weather.

"All the time," he answered. "I'm used to the heat, though."

The valet came around, and Tarence opened my door for me. I love a man with old school manners. We went by the mall in downtown Tampa to eat at Ocean Prime, but to his disappointment, they weren't open for lunch. They didn't open until five in the evening.

"We don't have a lot of time now. Do you mind just grabbing something over at the mall?" He pointed across the way. "There is a Cheesecake Factory if you like that."

"I don't mind at all," I said.

We started walking toward the mall entrance and approached the large grassy area we'd have to walk across.

"Uh, you don't think I'm going to walk across the grass in these heels on my own, do you?" I said to him.

He turned and grabbed my hand and helped me across the grassy pathway. We finally made it onto the mall property, but the journey wasn't over. In order to get to the Cheesecake Factory, we had to walk on a cobblestone path. Screw my life! That shit was even worse than walking on grass. One wrong step and I'd bust my ass.

"I should have worn my flats, sheesh," I said as I tried to tiptoe and not fall.

He grabbed my hand again. "Don't worry. I got you."

I don't know if it was the way he said it or if something just clicked, but I knew from that moment on this was a man who would know how to take care of me.

We walked the entire way holding hands. It was so pleasant. When we got inside the restaurant, we were escorted to a booth. I started clowning on this guy in there who looked like he was on *Men in Black* detail. I had Tarence cracking up. Neither of us had really looked at the menu because we were too busy laughing at each other and conversing. Our waiter came around twice and we still hadn't looked it over. The third time around, knowing time was of the essence, we finally ordered and enjoyed a good meal—and great company.

Tarence dropped me back at the hotel. Even then we sat outside in his car and talked for another twenty minutes or so. Once we got out of the car, we kissed and hugged each other so tight. I hadn't been flustered like that since God knows when. We leaned on his car just holding each other like a couple of teenagers in love. In my head, all I was thinking was how unexpected this was. One minute I was down and trying to support Rich in his time of need, and now I was floating on the clouds. What a difference twenty-four hours had made.

Within an hour, Rich and I were off to the airport. We boarded the plane and got all snug in our seats. Next we heard the captain's voice over the intercom.

"Ladies and gentlemen, unfortunately we've detected some minor mechanical issues with this Boeing 757. Though minor, it will take some time to fix. All passengers will have to de-board. Those with connecting flights, please see the flight attendant at the gate."

"Man, you've got to be shitting me." Rich said it, I said it, or we both said it. Either way, we found ourselves off the plane and back at the boarding gate, waiting to re-board. A half hour went by before we got word about our flight.

"Attention all passengers on flight 1089, your delayed flight to New York's JFK has now been cancelled."

There was such an outpouring of groans and sighs that I couldn't even hear what the announcer said next. We ended up getting rebooked to fly out the next day. The airline did agree to put us up at a hotel, though. You know how they say when life hands you lemons you should make lemonade? Let's just say that I added a little sugar to my lemonade by calling up Tarence and letting him know that what was probably bad news to everyone else on that flight was really good news for him and me.

"Dang, I feel bad, like this is my fault," he said over the phone when I called to tell him what had happened.

"Why?"

"Well, I kind of prayed to God and told Him that I didn't want you to have to go; that I wanted to spend a little bit more time with you." He sounded like a kid making a confession. "Guess God answers prayers after all." Look at God!

We both laughed.

"Looks like now we have another twenty-four hours to hang out," he said.

"Yeah, I guess it does kind of look that way, doesn't it?" I said, smiling through the phone.

"So, can I come scoop you up?"

He barely got to finish asking me the question before I let out a, "Hell yeah."

The airport had booked us two rooms in the hotel that was adjacent to the airport. As Rich and I were about to part ways to our rooms, he asked me, "What you gonna get into?"

"Oh, I'm just gon' chill and order room service," I lied, knowing my sneaky ass was dropping my bags and heading right back out to be with Tarence.

"All right then. I'll holler," Rich said as he disappeared behind his hotel room door.

Man, I dropped those bags off and flew back downstairs so fast. I walked outside of the hotel and met up with Tarence, who was driving his black Escalade.

"So nice to see you again so soon," I said after he'd gotten out of the car and opened my door for me.

"Right." He grinned then walked back around and got into the driver's seat. "What do you feel like doing?"

"I don't know. Is there anything good playing at the movies?"

"We can go by there and find out," he suggested.

"Sounds like a plan to me."

We'd just missed the beginning of the current showing, so we decided to have dinner and drinks while we waited for the next showing. When we got to the restaurant, there was a little bit of a wait, so we sat at the bar to have a drink until our table was ready.

"What can I get you two?" the bartender asked.

"I'll take a sour apple martini straight up, please," Tarence ordered.

"Wow, I used to drink that all the time. That sounds good right about now," I said to Tarence and then turned to the bartender. "I'll have the same thing, but you can put mine in a martini glass."

We talked more about our pasts, and it was refreshing to hear how honest Tarence was about his relationship before me.

"You were with your ex for seven years?" I asked. "Damn, that's a long time to be with someone. You guys never talked about marriage?"

"Naw."

"Why?"

"It just never came up," he replied.

Now, in my head I was like, *The hell you mean it just never came up?* Either ol' girl was nuts, or they were both stepping out on each other and just staying together because it was convenient. No way in hell I would be with a dude that long and the convo not come up at least once, twice, or seven times. Must be out your rabbit-ass mind. But again, I digress . . . LOL.

Anyway, we got seated at our table, enjoyed our dinner, and then went to the movies. The theater was right next door. We put our arms around each other's waists as we went up the escalators. I loved the fact that I was so much shorter than him. I felt so safe and cozy, nuzzled under shelter. His six feet and seven inches to my five feet and five inches was perfect in my book. Just being hugged up under him during the movie felt good too.

"Well, what would you like to do now, or are you ready to head back to the hotel?" Tarence asked me as we walked through the parking lot to his car after the movie.

"Nope, definitely do not need to go back to the hotel right now." I was hoping he couldn't tell I was blushing, because I was wearing one of my favorite MAC blushes as it was. I clutched onto him tightly, as if I never wanted to let him go, and as quiet as it's kept, I really didn't want to.

"Do you want to go back to my place? We can play pool and just relax. But I have to warn you: I live kind of far from here."

"It's okay," I told him. "I have an early flight, but what's a few more hours, right?"

He wasn't lying about the drive. We must have driven for an hour.

"Finally!" I said once we came to a stop at his place.

"I told you it was kind of far." He laughed.

"And you ain't never lied," I said. The street was very dark because he lived in a country area. All the houses were spread out, but his was lit up big and beautiful from the outside.

He opened the car door for me and led me into his place.

"This is really fly," I said.

"Well, thank you," he replied with that country twang I loved so much.

We entered through the garage. Upon walking in, I saw a long wet bar with dark counters, ivory leather bar stools. It had beige marble flooring throughout. I immediately remembered my mom's beige tile floor when I was a kid. Everything was elegant.

He brought me into the kitchen/living room area. I let out a gasp. "So we have the same color schemes going on in our living rooms?" I smirked. Half of his walls were white, with accents of a peachy and orange color, just like I had. I had ivory bar stools in my kitchen as well.

"Yeah?" he replied, shocked.

"We seem to be a bit connected here." I smiled.

As he continued to show me around his huge, beautifully decorated home, we came to his master bedroom.

Again I laughed. "Now this is scaring me."

"What now?"

"We got the same type of taste. This is nuts." He had tufted dark leather furniture, a huge sleigh bed, and one accent wall, just like my bedroom. The only difference was that his main wall was a turquoise kind of blue, and mine was olive green.

His bedroom ceiling was exceptionally high and painted in a gold sponged pattern. Just beautiful. Everything was beautiful. His foyer looked like something out of a Greek castle, with its tall columns and regal furnishings. The black grand piano in the corner topped everything off. The view from the foyer led out into his large outside patio and grill setup with a huge grotto-style pool. Just classy. I loved it all.

He took me upstairs to where the pool table was. It was outside, overlooking the pool. We played pool and talked again all night. I couldn't believe that three o'clock in the morning rolled around so quickly.

"You tired? You ready for me to go?" I asked him.

"Naw, I'm good," he said, yawning.

I knew we had a long ride back to the airport, so after a few minutes I asked him again if he was tired. I ended up getting the same response.

Man, I looked over at him five minutes later and he was passed out. I couldn't do anything but laugh. He was so darn cute.

I put a throw over him and watched television until he woke up. He was out for like forty-five minutes. He needed the rest.

"My bad. I can fall asleep anywhere at the drop of a dime. I was really trying to fight it."

"It's okay, sweetie. Like I said, I could tell you were tired. I don't know why you kept fighting it. Plus, you needed that nap since we got that long-ass drive back."

By the time he got me back to the hotel, it was five in the morning.

"At least we didn't pull a seven a.m. again," I said.

Once again we had to give our dreaded good-byes. I hated walking away from him. I hadn't enjoyed myself like that in a very, very, very long time. I found myself falling for him and didn't even think twice about it. It definitely crossed my mind that he could be the one. I mean, look how God had planned everything out for us to be able to be together. What started out as a business trip had definitely turned into pleasure, and I couldn't have cared less how that went against everything I'd set out to avoid.

God was still at work, because two weeks after that I had another event for an NBA player that Tarence was cool with. I called him and told him I had to make an appearance, and he asked if he could come. Blushing on the other end of the phone, I replied, "Of course you can come. That would be perfect!"

It was a celebrity event for Josh Howard in the Carolinas. I could not wait for that weekend to come so I could be in Tarence's presence again. We were all meeting at the first event, which was a flag football game, followed by pictures and an autograph-signing session. I had to leave the event during autographs because I had a performance that night in Greensboro, North Carolina for their summer jam concert.

Tarence and I were sitting at different ends of the autograph table signing, so I texted him that I had to leave but would be back after the show that night. He got up and walked out with me. So dayum sweet! He walked me to my waiting SUV, and we snuck in a quick kiss when Rich wasn't looking. Our budding romance was not a secret to Rich, but he didn't need to see me kissing my boo. Private moment over here, buddy.

It was a three-hour drive to my event, and I could not wait to get back to Tarence. After the performance, I slept during the drive back. I was worn out, but I knew once I was in Tarence's company, I'd be one hundred percent rejuvenated.

I was staying in the hotel where Josh was holding the wrap party for all of the weekend's events, but for some reason Tarence wasn't staying there. He assumed I was at his hotel, not where all the craziness was going down. By the time I got back to my hotel, it was raining and a bit cold out.

"Hey, boo, I just got back to the hotel. I am exhausted from that performance and ride back, so I am going to sit the party out," I told Tarence.

"That's cool, boo. I'll just come to you."

"Okay." I gave him my suite number.

"On my way," he said and then we ended the call.

I was so beat, I put on my Victoria's Secret blue and white T-shirt and a pair of matching pajama pants. I kept rubbing my eyes like sand was in them.

My phone rang and it was Tarence. "Hey, I'm here. Let me in."

I walked to the door and opened it, ready to squeeze his handsome ass so tight, but no one was on the other side of the door.

"Um, I just opened the door. I don't see anybody. Are you sure you're knocking on the right door?" I said as I closed my door.

"Yeah, you said seven-fifteen, right?"

"Yeah." I went and opened my door again. I looked at the number on the door to double check that I'd given him the right room number with my sleepy ass. "I have the door open, and I'm looking right at the numbers."

"Well, I'm standing right outside your door looking at the numbers seven-fifteen," he said. "Wait, what hotel are you at?"

"The same hotel Josh is at, where the party is. Are you not in this hotel?" I replied, all confused.

"Oh my God. I was there and left. I thought you were at my hotel. Damn it! And I sent the car service away. Ugh, I'm on my way back there."

We couldn't help but laugh. Obviously the hotel he was at was pretty close, because it was only about fifteen minutes before he was at my door. When I heard him knock, I flung the door open, still rubbing my tired eyes.

"Hey, baby," I said, noticing his clothes were kind of wet. "Did you get caught in the rain?"

"Man, I ran here from my hotel. I couldn't wait. The things I do for you." He was a bit out of breath.

I could not believe he had run in the rain just to come see about me. Only thing missing after that sentence was the Carl Thomas song "Summer Rain" playing in the background. Out of all the things, material and non-material, that men have done for me, this was by far the sweetest and the most romantic. On top of that, later that night he asked me old school if I would be his girlfriend. I said yes, and we have been inseparable ever since!

Tarence is more than I could have ever dreamed of. He's my real-life Prince Charming straight out of a Walt Disney story. What Tarence and I have is the kind of love that you don't mind working for. Because of our schedules, him playing basketball overseas and me singing and flying everywhere, you would think it would be a disaster, but you make time for the things you truly want. AND I WANT HIM FOREVER! I think it's safe for me to say that the feeling is mutual.

It's just so natural, so genuine. With Tarence I have learned that if love is done right, it will never hurt you a

day in your life. It just has to be with the right person—
and I believe I have found the right one for me.

I believe love is the best emotion in the universe. Kudos
to God for inventing this one!

Chapter 18

In the midst of me and Rich trying to get things popping off, an industry friend of mine by the name of Mona Scott Young e-mailed me. Her e-mail said for me to call her about a matter that was very important. I was wondering why she hadn't just called me, but then I realized that I changed my cell phone number every year. As artists, we have to change our numbers often. Sometimes fans get them, or you just have unwanted baggage calling you. So, if you were looking for me, you would have to tell a friend to tell a friend to reach me!

"Livy, my darling, how are you?" Mona said once I gave her a call.

"Hey, Mona. All is well. I can't complain. I hear you have been looking for the doll."

She laughed. "Yes, my love, I have. I want to run something by you and see if you would be interested."

"Okay, shoot. What is it?"

"Well, VH1 is developing this new show. It was originally called *Chrissy & Mr. Jones*. We want to change it around and bring in four women and make it like a *Sex and the City* reality show. Real fabulous women in the industry who are all connected in some way through their careers. Like, you would be the singer, Jim Jones's girl Chrissy, Puff's baby momma Misa Hylton, who we are looking at since she is a well-known stylist in industry."

"Yes, I know Misa very well. She dressed me for years while I was with G-Unit," I said.

"See, you guys have a connection already, Liv. And we are looking at this girl Emily, who is Fabolous's baby mother, and maybe Mashonda, who is the mother of Swizz Beats' son.

"So, what kind of show exactly is it, Mona? 'Cause you sound like you got a lot of different things going on. I don't wanna do anything messy," I said.

Mona said she wanted me to discuss 50 Cent. I didn't know how she would spin me and the girls taping, since I didn't know them, so I opted not to speak on 50 at all. You always gotta keep one eye open. When she brought up Fab the rapper, I had a red flag go up, and then Mashonda with the Swizz and Alicia drama . . . Shiiiiiit! Sounded like trouble to me.

"I don't know, Mona. It's sounding like it could get messy," I told her.

"No, no, it won't be like that. It's all about you women and how you make love and careers work with this male-driven hip hop industry. The things each and every one of you dealt with in the past. I mean, it's all new. We are trying to figure it out now. I just want to know if it's something you would be interested in; then we can all sit down with the network."

"Okay, Miss Mona. Set up a meeting."

I met with Mona and the people at VH1. We discussed the benefits of my doing the show.

"Liv, trust me. You guys are going to look like the black version of *Sex and the City*. We will follow your careers, partners, ups and downs, but it will all be done properly," Mona tried to assure me. I asked lots of questions and told them things I would be comfortable and not comfortable talking about.

"I'm not talking about G-Unit. If the show is about me, I don't want to bring them up, especially since none of them will be on the show," I told her. "Oh, and I ain't fighting nobody. I'm a lady, and we got goons to handle the messy stuff."

They all let out a laugh when I said that, but I was dead serious. Man, I had other projects pending, and if I was to do this show and look like a buffoon carrying on, these big endorsement companies would cut me off before I even got to the door. Who wants someone reppin' million-dollar companies if she looks like a clown on national television? I absolutely wouldn't want that. I always thought and planned ahead. I look for the bigger picture, not just for the "now."

"I don't have a problem with taping dates on the show, so I can work with you." I did have one last request. "You gotta show me in the studio, cutting my album. It should be about the music when I shoot my scenes." I was running down a list on them. So far Mona seemed to be in agreement with me and said that everything could be negotiated.

After that, Mona set up a meeting for me to meet Chrissy and Emily, because we didn't know each other. We met individually at the VH1 office. There were no cameras, just us, to see if we even would like each other, since they wanted us to tape as a group a lot. We hit it off well. The network loved our chemistry, and the rest was history.

The show did, though, end up having a very different premise when it was all said and done, but that is how *Love & Hip Hop* was born. That show truly helped me a lot during that period of my life, especially with getting my music to a broader audience. Most importantly, people would hopefully get the chance to see the real me. Sometimes I had to hope for the best once the episodes came out, because we never got to see the edits and the producers could spin things the way they wanted. We were all amateurs to this reality television thing during the first season. I just promised myself that no matter what situation they put me in, I wouldn't sell myself short for a camera look. I was going to be Olivia, and that was that. I was not into the buffoonery . . . no matter how much they paid me. Olivia Longott, not for sale, but always somehow having to pay the price.

Chapter 19

Rich appeared on *Love & Hip Hop* as well. Not only did he drive me crazy, but he would drive my best friend Jade nuts. Either he was calling to vent about me and my dating choices, or picking her brain about my music. Jade should have been getting paid for all the therapy hours she spent on the phone with Rich—as if listening to him and me go at it wasn't enough.

Rich and I bickered a lot actually. See, Rich was always right in his eyes. You couldn't tell him he wasn't the smartest person in the room. We used to beef about why I should open up more on the show, just letting the general public in, but I was built as a private person.

"Then at least get in the midst of more of the drama," Rich would tell me. "You need to start more arguments with castmates for ratings."

I'm not with all that fake shit. I shouldn't have to act like an asshole for people to buy my music, and I don't need to be an open book either. If this was the *Olivia Show*, then I could understand why I had to be so giving. What Rich had to remember was that first and foremost, I am an artist. I had not worked my ass off for years to be some joke of a TV personality, enjoy fifteen minutes of fame, and then never sell a record. I sing for a living. I have young girls who look up to me. I was about class and not trash. I'm trying to get big endorsements, and those companies who hand out those big checks aren't giving Bonquisha who acts a fool on *Love & Hip Hop* a check to endorse Colgate! I always think ahead—another nugget 50 passed on to me.

With Rich now on my team, things were starting to look up. I just prayed he would deliver and not disappoint me. Rich and I worked well together, and it had always been one hundred percent business. For one, I had just gotten out of a relationship, and for two, just like his name says, when it came to me, Rich knew we could definitely make those "dollaz" together. And last but not least, wasn't nobody was trying to holla at Rich's ass. I called him "Dadager" for a reason. I saw him as a father figure.

It has felt like a long two years with Rich Dollaz, but it was worth all the road trips, all the late and early flights, and all those interviews, because everything was part of a plan. Rich and I had a goal to meet: to make the non-believers believe again, and for those who always believed to keep believing.

The hardest part was convincing the labels. Rich took every meeting by himself. I can recall going to about two meetings with him, and those were with execs I already had a rapport with. When I say Rich sat with almost every label executive known to man, I'm not exaggerating.

Each one had their own reasons why they couldn't work with me. Either it was that I was asking for too much money—even though they were really trying to lowball me on the numbers because they mistook me for a desperate chick—or they wanted us to put out a record first and work it ourselves to see how the general public reacted to me. Rich believed in me, and I believed in myself too much for that nonsense.

"Yo, Liv. You know what?" Rich said to me one day. "Let's put out a record and show these idiots how the fuck we do."

I honestly hadn't really thought about that. My goal from the time I knew this was what I wanted to do in life was to get a record deal and let the label put my work out. But Rich was hype. He was a radio guy, so he was one-hundred percent sure of what he could do as far as putting me out there and getting me spins. He had no doubts that we could produce a record and get the necessary radio play to let the public know what I was really about.

"You know what?" I said to Rich, nodding my head. "Let's do the damn thing. You're right. I'm dying to stick it to these meatballs," I said with conviction. So, he found some new up and coming producers and brought me the track for "December."

At this time I was filming *Love & Hip Hop*, so Rich thought we could capitalize more by recording it on the show. We showed a little bit of the studio process and a clip of me singing the hook, and we were off to the races.

Rich had already sent the record to radio stations, and we were getting a lot of good feedback. Since we were doing this independently, I gave Rich half of the money from my shows to keep the record up and running. In a week, the "December" music video had over one million views on YouTube. I charted on Billboard's top 100 without a label. I peaked at number thirty-two. On the iTunes R&B chart, I was top ten. "December" hit the number two and then the number one spot.

The single was a smash! Everywhere I performed the record, I could just hold the mic out and the audience sang it word for word. Man, I was getting back that good feeling. With all the publicity on radio, TV, and the internet, I was sure Rich could get me the record deal I wanted. But the labels wanted more. They tried to tell him the only reason the record did so well was because I was on the show, not because of my talent.

Can you believe that? All that hard work and it still wasn't good enough?

"Man, they need to go somewhere with that BS excuse," I told Rich.

So, we set out once again to prove the public loved me and that it wasn't just the luck of the draw. This time we put out a record called "Walk Away." I recorded it in Atlantic City with these two producers named Chris and Teeb. Just like with "December," "Walk Away" took off. I didn't just stop there. I did another record called "Where Do I Go from Here," while doing the *Love & Hip Hop* show. I pretty much did that out of spite. I didn't even want to do the record, but I had something to prove.

"Where Do I Go From Here" did great.

"Now, what the hell else do I have to do to show these labels that I'm deserving of a proper deal?" I asked Rich.

There were deals offered to me, but they weren't sufficient enough for what I wanted. If I've said it once, I'll say it a thousand more times: I know my worth. Some people say I should have taken the deals, but I was not comfortable settling. This would have been my third deal, so I had to be sure. One wrong move by being at the wrong label could finish my career. I had to choose wisely, so I chose to wait. Because I decided to turn down the deals that were offered to me, I had to hear, "Well, she's just a diva. She thinks she's better than she really is."

Everyone swore they knew me and what was going on inside my head—and my heart. Everyone knew my sound, or what I should have been singing, or how I should be acting, but none of them really knew me, the real Olivia. Everyone was working off of word of mouth. When we went into meetings with great music, they seemed to be in awe and always hit me with the, "Oh my God, that's you singing?"

"Of course it's me!" I wanted to scream so many times. It just became so annoying, and to some degree, hurtful. All this time I'd been as real as real could get, and yet they were basically telling me to my face they thought I was a phony.

What people didn't know is usually I do my own hair and makeup (yes, even for shows). That is another craft I have always been good at. Rich and I basically had to go back and fix all the false crap people thought was me so that they could see the real me. It was all just so draining. I felt like I was on trial, being accused of something I didn't do, so I had to defend myself tooth and nail. But did the jury believe me?

At times I would just break, and unfortunately Rich would have to endure the brunt of it.

"It's cold out here, Liv," he would say, "But I promise you I'm dedicating my every waking moment to trying to fix all the old bullshit."

"I don't understand what the fucking problem is. All these non-talented artists are out here copping deals. Even if they are bad deals, they still getting offered something. Why do I gotta fucking jump through hoops? I'm tired of this shit." I think I said everything in one breath.

"Calm down, Liv. I'm going to fix it. It can be fixed. You're a fuckin gold mine. Trust me. I will get you the deal you want. I won't stop until I do," he said, trying to lower my pressure, which was clearly up. "I'm on your team. I want you to win."

"I know, Rich. It's just that I need a shot. Just one more shot." When I ended that call with Rich, I got a shot all right—of Patrón. I hate to admit it, but a lot of times, that's just where I would find myself after all the bullshit in the music game.

Thank God Rich didn't have to deal with too many outbursts like that from me. Lucky for him, I'd taught myself early on to be very self-reliant and keep things to myself. Well, I don't actually keep everything to myself. I tell God everything, of course. Prayer and faith have always been my best friends. I'd be lost without them. And without fail, God continued to answer my prayers and give me a sign that I was still on the right path.

I had no idea *Love & Hip Hop* was going to be the huge success that it turned out to be. I don't think anyone ever does. You just pray that it works. Doing the show allowed my fans to see the struggle, to see the rise and fall and rise again.

Most people will never understand what someone in the entertainment industry goes through, the things we cope with, how we learn to deal with these issues, and what it does to a person. Whenever you put yourself out there in the spotlight, it's like carrying a cross and waiting to see if anyone is going to nail you to it. People will tear you down on purpose, just so they can put themselves in a position to say that they are the one who built you back up.

As artists, we endure it because we love our craft and we love our fans. You have to want to be a people pleaser to be in this business. Fans are truly the wind beneath your wings, the air you breathe. It doesn't matter what you've gone through or how bad a day you had; when you hit that stage, they breathe new life into you. They resuscitate you, in a sense.

Meanwhile, you have people in the background just waiting to suck the life right back out of you.

In the end, though, I'm still fighting for what I believe in, and will continue to push forward, because I know my purpose. An author named E. N. Joy once said, "The greatest 'ah-ha moment' a person can have is when their life begins to make sense." Well, people, for the first time in my life, I can honestly say that it's all starting to make sense.

From the Author

When are you too old to stop dreaming, and who says you ever have to stop? Everyone has a dream. A dream of love, careers, world peace, hope, fortune, happiness . . . Whatever your dreams may be, do not—I repeat, do not—let anyone crush them! Your faith should be bigger than your fears. You never want to go through life with regret.

Always dream big and be able to say you tried to obtain your dreams. I can recall as a little girl wanting to be a pediatrician because I just loved babies. Then when I started to realize I could sing, my mom said, "Well, why don't you become a singing pediatrician?" Oh my goodness, we used to laugh at my mom all the time for that suggestion. But once I made up my mind that singing was the dream I wanted to achieve, I never looked back, and I have been living out my dreams ever since.

What will you give, and how far will you go to achieve your dreams? A lot of people think their dreams have to end because they had a child too soon, or because they are too old, or just plain don't believe in themselves anymore. Everyone has something they regret not trying in life. It could be that you never finished school, or put your career on hold to raise a child or have a family. Or maybe you didn't have the funds to open your own business but never really went out and tried to achieve that goal.

Why do you think you put your plans on the back burner to begin with? Once you figure that out, you have taken the first step. What I truly don't understand is why people don't wholeheartedly believe in themselves. Many people will doubt you, some because they are jealous or wish they had gone after their dreams, or else they are just plain haters. You have to dig deep and realize why you were put on this earth. It is as simple as knowing what you are great at. It could just be a hobby, it could be something so small that you are overlooking it as being your possible calling.

Let me give you an example. I have this best friend who is absolutely amazing at cooking. Libbe is *amazing*. She loves to be in the kitchen. She's the type of person who takes pride in her food and presentation just so we can enjoy a gourmet meal. Now, get this: She knows she is a great cook, so why not go to culinary school? Why not start your own business? Start catering parties or something? Sounds so simple, right? Well, I believe she puts it off because she is afraid of failing. What she doesn't realize is that we all have to fall in order to figure out what we are good at—and if you are truly gifted at something, you won't fail. You will never know unless you try. We all have to make a few mistakes in order to get to the next step. How else will you know if it works or not? For all I know my friend could be afraid to succeed.

Some people put a limit on themselves. I personally have many things that I still want to accomplish. It doesn't stop at music with me. That's just what I chose to start with. What will you choose to start with? For God's sake, start with something! Sky's the limit, right? Nope. It's just the view.

ORDER FORM
URBAN BOOKS, LLC
97 N18th Street
Wyandanch, NY 11798

Name (please print):_____

Address: _____

City/State: _____

Zip: _____

QTY	TITLES	PRICE
	16 On The Block	$14.95
	A Girl From Flint	$14.95
	A Pimp's Life	$14.95
	Baltimore Chronicles	$14.95
	Baltimore Chronicles 2	$14.95
	Betrayal	$14.95
	Bi-Curious	$14.95
	Bi-Curious 2: Life After Sadie	$14.95
	Bi-Curious 3: Trapped	$14.95
	Both Sides Of The Fence	$14.95
	Both Sides Of The Fence 2	$14.95
	California Connection	$14.95

Shipping and handling: add $3.50 for 1st book, then $1.75 for each additional book.
Please send a check payable to:
Urban Books, LLC
Please allow 4-6 weeks for delivery

ORDER FORM
URBAN BOOKS, LLC
97 N18th Street
Wyandanch, NY 11798

Name (please print):_____

Address: _____

City/State: _____

Zip: _____

QTY	TITLES	PRICE
	California Connection 2	$14.95
	Cheesecake And Teardrops	$14.95
	Congratulations	$14.95
	Crazy In Love	$14.95
	Cyber Case	$14.95
	Denim Diaries	$14.95
	Diary Of A Mad First Lady	$14.95
	Diary Of A Stalker	$14.95
	Diary Of A Street Diva	$14.95
	Diary Of A Young Girl	$14.95
	Dirty Money	$14.95
	Dirty To The Grave	$14.95

Shipping and handling: add $3.50 for 1st book, then $1.75 for each additional book.
Please send a check payable to:
Urban Books, LLC
Please allow 4-6 weeks for delivery

ORDER FORM
URBAN BOOKS, LLC
97 N18th Street
Wyandanch, NY 11798

Name (please print):_____

Address: _____

City/State: _____

Zip: _____

QTY	TITLES	PRICE
	Gunz And Roses	$14.95
	Happily Ever Now	$14.95
	Hell Has No Fury	$14.95
	Hush	$14.95
	If It Isn't love	$14.95
	Kiss Kiss Bang Bang	$14.95
	Last Breath	$14.95
	Little Black Girl Lost	$14.95
	Little Black Girl Lost 2	$14.95
	Little Black Girl Lost 3	$14.95
	Little Black Girl Lost 4	$14.95
	Little Black Girl Lost 5	$14.95

Shipping and handling: add $3.50 for 1st book, then $1.75 for each additional book.
Please send a check payable to:
Urban Books, LLC
Please allow 4-6 weeks for delivery

ORDER FORM
URBAN BOOKS, LLC
97 N18th Street
Wyandanch, NY 11798

Name (please print):_____

Address: _____

City/State: _____

Zip: _____

QTY	TITLES	PRICE
	Loving Dasia	$14.95
	Material Girl	$14.95
	Moth To A Flame	$14.95
	Mr. High Maintenance	$14.95
	My Little Secret	$14.95
	Naughty	$14.95
	Naughty 2	$14.95
	Naughty 3	$14.95
	Queen Bee	$14.95
	Say It Ain't So	$14.95
	Snapped	$14.95
	Snow White	$14.95

Shipping and handling: add $3.50 for 1st book, then $1.75 for each additional book.
Please send a check payable to:
    Urban Books, LLC
Please allow 4-6 weeks for delivery